M

Jean Morrow, Series Editor

1. *Music Classification Systems*, by Mark McKnight, edited by Linda Barnhart, 2002.
2. *Binding and Care of Printed Music*, by Alice Carli, 2003.
3. *Music Library Instruction*, by Gregg S. Geary, Laura M. Snyder, and Kathleen A. Abromeit, edited by Deborah Campana, 2004.

Music Library Instruction

Gregg S. Geary
Laura M. Snyder
Kathleen A. Abromeit

Edited by
Deborah Campana

MLA Basic Manual Series, No. 3

The Scarecrow Press, Inc.
Lanham, Maryland • Toronto • Oxford
2004

SCARECROW PRESS, INC.

Published in the United States of America
by Scarecrow Press, Inc.
A wholly owned subsidiary of
The Rowman & Littlefield Publishing Group, Inc.
4501 Forbes Boulevard, Suite 200, Lanham, Maryland 20706
www.scarecrowpress.com

PO Box 317
Oxford
OX2 9RU, UK

Copyright © 2004 by Music Library Association

All rights reserved. No part of this publication may be reproduced, stored in a retrieval system, or transmitted in any form or by any means, electronic, mechanical, photocopying, recording, or otherwise, without the prior permission of the publisher.

British Library Cataloguing in Publication Information Available

Library of Congress Cataloging-in-Publication Data

Geary, Gregg S.
  Music library instruction / Gregg S. Geary, Laura M. Snyder, Kathleen A. Abromeit ; edited by Deborah Campana.
    p. cm.—(Music Library Association basic manual series ; no. 3)
  Includes bibliographical references (p.   ) and index.
  ISBN 0-8108-5002-8 (paperback : alk. paper)
  1. Music librarianship. 2. Music—Bibliography. 3. Library orientation for college students. I. Snyder, Laura M. II. Abromeit, Kathleen A., 1962– III. Campana, Deborah Ann. IV. Title. V. Series.
ML111 .G42 2004
025.5'6678—dc22
                                                                    2003023007

Manufactured in the United States of America.

Contents

Introduction   vii

1   Creating Information Literacy Instruction for Undergraduates in the Music Library   1
Gregg S. Geary

2   Teaching the Graduate Music Research Course   47
Laura M. Snyder

3   Reference Assistants on the Front Line in the Music Library   99
Kathleen A. Abromeit

Index   131

About the Authors and Editor   137

Introduction

In general, music librarians are not trained to teach, and yet many find themselves in front of the classroom instructing on all facets of database use to research strategies in musicology. How can one develop effective teaching techniques or design curricula so that the initial classroom opportunity can be a success? The expertise detailed in this volume on music library instruction imparts three perspectives on this issue.

Although determining when librarians began offering group instruction to their users is impossible, one indicator of such widespread offerings is the establishment of the Association of College and Research Libraries' Bibliographic Instruction Section (BIS) in 1978. A few years later in 1982, the number of instructional programs in midwestern music libraries was documented in the MLA Midwest Chapter's publication, "A Directory of Instruction Programs in the Midwest," and by 1984, the same MLA chapter published in *Notes* "Bibliographic Competencies for Music Students at an Undergraduate Level," which contained a detailed listing of "library skills . . . essential to any undergraduate course of study."[1]

Bibliographic instruction (or BI) in music libraries initially centered on teaching groups of students primarily in academic programs about music resources. At the same time, library online systems were still fairly new and public interfaces had evolved to such a degree that instruction became necessary for the average user to actually make use of a collection. These instructional programs did not supplant the need for one-to-one contact of the reference setting, but at the very least allowed librarians to introduce the mechanics of the online system as well as the most important music reference resources. They also represented a paradigm shift in determining what libraries needed to offer their users.

A decade later saw the continued proliferation of digital resources including the World Wide Web, available to the general public and surpassing all expectations for educational use. When users were able to conduct research on their home computers beyond the confines of the library, the need for instructional intervention grew more acute. Not only were students able to access resources on their own time in locations away from the aid of librarians, there were many more and varied resources from which to choose. A student without adequate training and background could mistakenly interpret John Q. Public's personal web page as authoritative as an online encyclopedia accessible via the library's web pages. Library users no longer merely required answers to their questions, they needed to develop the critical apparatus to evaluate the information they found and discover how they should go about finding it. Although the bibliographic competencies stated in the 1984 *Notes* article were still valid, librarians reconsidered users' needs. Not only did users require an understanding of basic resources, but they needed to evaluate the quality and usefulness of resources encountered on a daily basis, to develop an "information literacy,"[2] an approach that is still vital today.

MLA's Basic Manual Series intends to present definitive discussion on specific aspects of the music library profession, but this volume differs from others in the series. Although it focuses uniquely on instruction in the music library, because music library users' needs, curricular content, or institutional designs differ, it would be impossible to present a single viewpoint on this subject. Moreover, because the nature of such instructional programs meshes intimately with the institution itself, to divorce a program from its library would negate the context for its development. As a result, this volume provides three different approaches to instructional programs.

Gregg Geary demonstrates how plans for teaching nonmusic majors about music resources match educational competencies established at the University of Hawaii; Laura Snyder presents the course she helped develop while teaching a graduate-level class on music bibliography at Eastman; and Kathleen Abromeit offers an overview of the program employed at Oberlin Conservatory Library for training undergraduate students to serve as reference assistants. Hopefully, readers will identify with the traits of these programs, adapt ideas applicable to their own settings, and ultimately benefit from the experiences of these authors. We are happy to recognize their work, along with that of Suzanne Temple, member services librarian, Fenway Libraries Online, who indexed this volume.

Deborah Campana, editor

NOTES

1. "Bibliographic Competencies for Music Students at an Undergraduate Level." *Notes* 40 (March 1984): 529–32.

2. Amanda Maple, Beth Christensen, and Kathleen A. Abromeit, "Information Literacy for Undergraduate Music Students: A Conceptual Framework," *Notes* 52 (March 1996): 745.

1

Creating Information Literacy Instruction for Undergraduates in the Music Library

Gregg S. Geary

INTRODUCTION

Twenty-five years ago, the academic librarian had a much different job than the one faced by librarians today. The increased use of technology has had a great impact on the organization of the library and the type of services it provides. Foremost among the changes in services is the increased instruction librarians must offer users in order to help patrons meet the changing technological landscape. Job descriptions for academic librarians now frequently require experience in library instruction as a minimum or desired qualification for employment.[1]

Music librarian positions are no exception. In an age of specialization, the academic music librarian often enters the profession anticipating a career filled exclusively with research into the field of music. If thoughts of bibliographic instruction are entertained, the music librarian may anticipate a class of ten or twelve music graduate students eager to explore the location of early imprints through works like *Répertoire International des Sources Musicales (RISM)*, or to look for an obscure chamber work by a long forgotten composer listed in Pazdirek's *Universal-Handbuch der Musikliteratur*. But, as is so often the case, reality paints a somewhat different picture of the library setting.

The music librarian often finds that the graduate classes in music bibliography are the domain of the musicologist. This often closes that avenue of instruction for the music librarian except for the occasional guest lecture on the latest online product. In addition, with stretched budgets, multitasking, team building and cross training becoming the norm among today's librarians, the music librarian is often required to perform tasks outside the traditional areas of responsibility.

It is not uncommon for the music librarian to be called upon to offer bibliographic instruction or information literacy classes to music and nonmusic majors. But how, one may ask, is this best done? Should the music librarian copy the approach taken by the general reference librarian? Should he or she leave behind the detailed knowledge of music information resources they know so well? This chapter answers these questions with a resounding "no." Granted, the music librarians who need to instruct nonmusicians must make some accommodations and expand their knowledge of general information resources, but this is to the good of both students and music librarians. It is also true, however, that the nonmusician can learn the essential concepts of information literacy by using music-specific information resources.

Consider also, the fact that many music librarians, indeed, most librarians of any description, lack specific training in the methods of classroom teaching, save for those whose background is in education. Curriculum design, which is so much a part of training in education, is often not a part of graduate programs in either library science or musicology. Yet a thorough knowledge of course designs, assessment, and various other classroom techniques are a great help to those who must provide library instruction.

This chapter is neither a substitute for a methods class in education nor a book on teaching techniques. It does, however, present some techniques and approaches gleaned from a review of the library and curriculum design literature and practical experience. Hopefully this information can aid academic music librarians in meeting the challenges of information literacy instruction for both music and nonmusic undergraduates.

BACKGROUND

There are a number of different teaching venues for academic librarians. These include:

- One-on-one instruction (via reference desk assistance or other consultation settings)
- Print and online tutorials
- One-shot lectures conducted in the library or as part of a regularly scheduled class
- Mini courses that link to regularly scheduled classes
- Semester-long classes in library instruction

Subject specialists, such as music librarians, are often asked to make presentations to music classes, usually at the graduate level, to introduce a core repertoire of music reference sources particular to the needs of a single class. But, as stated earlier, the music librarian cannot expect to have this venue as their sole teaching outlet. While this discussion will speak to the merits of the semester-long course as an excellent way to provide quality instruction, the techniques presented here are easily adaptable to any teaching venue.

Much of the practical material presented in this chapter stems from teaching experiences in undergraduate instruction for both music and nonmusic majors at the University of Hawaii at Manoa.[2] The music faculty and music librarian recognized that music research skills at the undergraduate level were markedly lacking. After years of teaching one-shot lectures to upper-level undergraduate and graduate classes it was thought that development of a semester-long course for sophomores would be a simple task. But this was not the case. Patterning undergraduate library instruction after a graduate music research class was not effective in producing information literate undergraduate students. It was the wrong instructional model. What was really needed was a new approach that focused on the unique demands of information literacy. Previous models emphasized detailed content rather than the larger concepts essential to developing lifelong information gathering skills.

The primary lesson learned during the years of course development and refinement is that teaching information literacy requires a shift away from introducing a core repertoire of music reference tools to a focus on core competencies that stress information literacy. The trick is to use the competencies to organize the material in new ways. Some of the standard music reference tools can be used, but they are used as examples of a type of information resource. The broader nature of the resource and its organization should be stressed rather than its specific application for music research. While it may seem modest at first, this shift makes an important difference pedagogically.

LESSONS AND PRACTICAL ADVICE

One of the most useful tools in grappling with teaching information literacy is identifying a list of competencies that each information literate student should possess. These competencies influence all the teaching and activities planned for any bibliographic instruction. The sections below will identify the competencies that lead to information literacy, provide tips on organizing curriculum and developing a syllabus, provide examples of library assignments, and present a variety of assessment methods.

The Competencies

The library instruction literature currently provides a number of lists of information literacy competencies that students should possess to function in our information-rich and highly technological society. The Association of College and Research Libraries (ACRL) provides an exceptional website on information literacy that includes a detailed list of competency standards for higher education.[3] Many such lists are invaluable as a starting point in developing an information literacy program.

This chapter relies on a list of competencies developed in 1997 at the University of Hawaii. While having many elements in common with other lists of information literacy competencies, this list has the distinction of identifying general competencies (skills learned) and affective competencies (student reactions to learning the skills). Focusing on the competencies listed below can provide a new perspective on presenting music information resources. They can help the instructor see music resources as models of their genre and stress the essential qualities they share with other similar reference works in other fields. The great advantage to this view is that it prepares students for lifelong learning. For example, when focused on the competencies, the music librarian does not just teach students how to use the *New Grove Dictionary of Music and Musicians,* 2nd ed. (*NG2*), but instead teaches them to use any encyclopedia. A conscious effort is made to remind students that *NG2* shares many important qualities with other encyclopedias; these qualities should be listed in all assignments and reviewed in class. Texts such as *Guide to the Use of Libraries and Information Sources* by Jean Gates are well designed to support this type of instruction.[4]

When comparing the *NG2* to other encyclopedias, students should be able to compare and contrast criteria such as organization, authority, writing style, ease of use, and special features. Students should also be able to discuss when these different resources are best used. Such analysis and evaluation of an information resource is an essential part of the critical thinking process.[5] These activities promote information seeking strategies (competency 2) and critical and evaluative thinking (competency 7). Nothing in this is essentially new, but for those music librarians with years of music research experience and in-depth musicological training it is not always easy to see the big picture the undergraduate needs. This is especially true of the undergraduate who is studying music as an elective or is not a music major.

As stated earlier, all the competencies in the list below possess both a general and an affective aspect. The general competency identifies the objective skill the student should perform and the affective competency identifies the subjective emotional response the student should achieve. This dualism provides a more holistic approach to library instruction that recognizes that student's emotional responses affect their performance.[6] So much attention is usually focused on the development of research skills it is easy to lose sight of the emotional state of the student. Carolyn Kuhlthau's research into the information search process also recognizes the importance of feelings as students pass through the six stages of her search process model.[7]

LIBRARY INSTRUCTION COMPETENCIES

Developed by the Librarians of the Central Information Services Business, Humanities & Social Sciences Department, Hamilton Library, University of Hawaii at Manoa
(Adopted 4/97. Used by permission)

General Competency 1: Task Definition

I. User can recognize, identify, and define an information need.
   A. User can articulate an information need that:
      1. Identifies key concepts of the information need.
      2. Identifies synonymous words for key concepts.
      3. Identifies words for narrowing the scope of an information need that require exploration.
      4. Identifies words for broadening the scope of an information need by determining contextual issues that require exploration.
   B. User can distinguish between the need for concrete factual information from the need for opinion information.

C. User can determine the relevant time period or date of publication for the information need.
D. User can determine primary and secondary information source requirements.
E. User can determine when an information need is discipline specific or interdisciplinary.

Affective Competency 1: Task Definition

User is comfortable discussing their information need with a librarian or going directly to the access resources.

General Competency 2: Information Seeking Strategies

I. User can recognize the range of information sources in terms of function, format, organizational content, and bibliographic structure.
   A. User can define the general information provision role of books, reference books, journals, magazines, newspapers, government publications, video recordings, listservs, and online data sources.
   B. User can determine what category of information resource is most relevant to the information need.
   C. User recognizes the importance of title, thesis, preface, introduction, table of contents, appendixes, summary and/or abstract in determining the scope, limitations, and special feature of information sources and thereby their usefulness.
II. User understands how information sources are bibliographically structured.
   A. User can identify the elements of a record (citation).
   B. User can identify elements of records (citations) called access points which correspond to the information need as the most pertinent for finding a source.

C. User recognizes that the form of a record (citation) varies for different disciplines, subject areas, or databases while retaining common elements.

Affective Competency 2: Information Seeking Strategies

Users have confidence that they can determine the appropriate category of information resources.

General Competency 3: Location and Access of Information Sources

I. User understands that there are access tools whose primary purpose is to identify information sources.
   A. User understands that no access tool is comprehensive in scope.
   B. User recognizes that access tools vary by the type of information sources needed.
   C. User recognizes that access tools vary by discipline or subject area.
   D. User recognizes that access tools vary in format and recognizes the implications of format as it relates to the availability of access points.
   E. User can determine the appropriate access tool for the information need.

Affective Competency 3: Location and Access of Information Sources

User is at ease in selecting an access tool.

General Competency 4: Location and Access within Electronic Information Sources

I. User can determine what access points can be utilized within specific electronic access tools.

A. User understands keyword searching.
B. User understands Boolean connectors.
C. User understands truncation.
D. User understands controlled vocabulary searching.
E. User understands proximity searching.

Affective Competency 4: Location and Access within Electronic Information Sources

Users have confidence in their ability to select appropriate access points.

General Competency 5: Hardware and Software Knowledge

I. User can identify standard computer hardware and software structures.
   A. User knows relevant keyboard and browser functions (e.g., enter/return key, backspace key, function keys, print key or print protocol, and use of hotlinks, back, forward, and stop button found in web browsers).
   B. User knows function of mouse vs. keyboard.
   C. User can identify and use menu screens.
   D. User can identify and use basic commands.
   E. User can exit/quit a system or database.
   F. User can start a new search or database.
   G. User can execute print protocol.
   H. User can start a new web browser and navigate in it effectively.
   I. User can execute online help.

Affective Competency 5: Hardware and Software Knowledge

User feels in control when using command options and trusts the reliability of standard commands and keyboard options.

General Competency 6: Library Physical Organization and Collection

I. User understands the library's physical organization, location of collections, and procedures.
   A. User understands that libraries may group information sources by subject, author, call number, format, publisher, type of material, or special audience.
   B. User can identify which organization technique has been used for the group of information sources relevant to an information need.
   C. User can identify and locate which collections are most relevant to their information need.

Affective Competency 6: Library Physical Organization and Collection

User has confidence in his or her ability to find information sources in the library.

General Competency 7: Evaluation and Critical Thinking

I. User can evaluate the usefulness and appropriateness of information resources.
   A. User can determine the relevance of currency to an information need in the context of the publication record of that need.
   B. User understands the difference between primary and secondary sources in information and can determine their relevance to an information need.
   C. User understands that individuals or groups identify themselves as belonging to specific areas and/or disciplines.
   D. User can determine whether an information resource is scholarly or popular.
   E. User understands the relevance of author expertise to the sources of information being used.

F. User recognizes that disciplines use specific methods to communicate information and determine "truth."
G. User recognizes when a topic or issue is discipline specific or interdisciplinary.
H. User understands the nature of discourse on a subject and can place selected sources in the context of that discourse.
I. User can identify search strategies to gather information relevant to evaluating selected information resources.

Affective Competency 7: Evaluation and Critical Thinking

User feels confident that he or she can evaluate the located information.

Addressing all these competencies, even in a three-credit course, is a challenge. Some competencies take more time than others to develop. Some students will already possess some of these competencies and others will possess none. Careful attention to these competencies will, however, prove invaluable as a guide in developing specific goals for class instruction. Developing strategies and methodologies that will lead students to master these competencies depends largely upon the imagination, creativity, and experience of the music librarian. There is no one road to success in teaching information literacy, whether using music materials or any other body of knowledge. This chapter, and the resources listed in the bibliography, can only provide a point of entry to this field and some basic advice. Each music librarian must find the approach that fits his or her personality and unique gifts.

The seven Cs of information literacy listed below attempt to summarize many of the elements in the list of competencies and identify the desired qualities instructors should develop in student researchers. The items on the list are gleaned from the information literacy literature and years of experience. It also seeks to combine both the objective and affective components of information literacy. Other useful lists are readily available in the library instruction literature.[8]

THE SEVEN Cs OF INFORMATION LITERACY

An information literate student should be:

1. *Curious* about the world, inquisitive, seeking truth.
2. *Comfortable* using a wide variety of information tools.
3. *Creative* in applying their information skills.
4. *Competent* in using information tools.
5. *Confident* of their ability to gather information appropriately.
6. *Critical* in their thinking (questioning and evaluating).
7. *Contributing* to the body of knowledge by effectively sharing what they learn from their research both orally and in writing.

Developing the Syllabus

The syllabus is one of the best places to start in developing a class. It is the place to plan and establish the class objectives, content, organization, assessments, and strategies for teaching. As a music librarian, this is the place to decide which music resources will best suit the development of the information competencies students need. The process of developing the syllabus is the time to reflect on what really needs to be taught and consider how best to teach it. While a one-shot class session does not require a syllabus, it still requires the same careful planning.

A good syllabus should:

- Establish the course objectives.
- Identify the competencies to be taught.
- Identify the information resources, including music resources, which will be used to teach the skills and competencies.
- Organize the resources for presentation in a logical and systematic fashion.
- Estimate the time needed to teach, practice, and assess each skill or competency.
- Identify how student performance will be assessed.

Some of these issues will depend on individual students' learning styles and the class group dynamic. This means that no matter how carefully a syllabus is planned, the instructor must remain flexible and be prepared to make appropriate changes. Some instructors present a brief syllabus while others are more detailed. The time invested in creating a more detailed syllabus is repaid many times by minimizing confusion and misunderstandings between teacher and students. In addition, since the music librarian may also be teaching nonmusicians who might be apprehensive about their lack of subject knowledge, the syllabus can be a place to allay any fears and clarify any misapprehensions.

Those new to classroom instruction should review the library instruction literature to help identify best practices and study proven techniques. Draw together a number of resources before going too far. The bibliography at the end of this chapter supplies several helpful resources. Do not be limited to only the most recent publications. Many pre-Internet publications supply useful information on the research process. They are easily adapted to serve the objectives of modern information literacy. Also, do not be limited to material written for the college teacher. Many works on information literacy intended for elementary or high school instructors are particularly valuable in developing relevant material for freshmen. It is useful to remember that freshmen are only high school seniors back from summer vacation. Material designed for younger audiences can help the music librarian, who may be accustomed to working with graduate students, avoid setting expectations that are unreasonable for freshmen. *Information Power: Building Partnerships for Learning* prepared by the American Association of School Librarians and the Association for Educational Communications and Technology is a notable example. This work, designed for elementary and secondary instructors, contains concepts, analysis, recommendations and outstanding documentation that make it equally applicable to post-secondary instruction. This is not a case of "dumbing down" the college curriculum. The content an academic librarian deals with should certainly challenge the students. But it is often the case that the school librarian literature provides practical insights into the teaching and learning process that can be a great help to academic librarians.

Writing the Objectives

The course objectives provide the framework for creating a class and should be included in the syllabus. These are the "big ideas" that influence the entire course design. Every lecture, every exercise, every assignment, must further the course objectives. There must always be a direct correlation between every activity a student performs and the course objectives. Instructors all too easily forget this, especially if the instructor does not "own" the course objectives. This may occur when the course objectives are either not devised by the instructor or that he or she does not believe in them passionately. Objectives that are handed down from previous instructors, administrators, or the college catalog must be set aside and reexamined. A good test would be to see if the objectives incorporate goals that appear in the list of information literacy competencies or the seven Cs of information literacy. Samples of course objective statements include:

- Provide students with the essential information gathering concepts and skills foundational to all future research.
- Aid students to become critical and confident users of libraries and other information resources.
- Help students master essential information gathering skills and apply them appropriately to support a thesis.
- Help students build research and information gathering skills through the use of music-related resources.

An instructor must believe in these course objectives and be dedicated to their achievement. If instructors do not "buy in" to these objectives their teaching soon becomes a dull routine.

Gathering the Resources

Great care must be given to choosing the resources that will become part of the instructional design. Because the field of music is fortunate to have many fine reference works of great quality, it is easy to try and fit too many resources into the curriculum. In designing a course in information literacy the rule is "less is more." This dictum extends to all teaching venues, from the one-shot lecture to the three-credit course. Always ask, "What competencies are essential for all students to know, not just today, but five, ten or twenty years hence?" Then locate the music-related information tools that best illustrate those competencies.

It will not be difficult to identify a music resource to match every competency required. The library literature contains many resources that list general and music-specific reference materials along with discussions of the research process. Such works have been in print long before information literacy became a buzzword for librarians. Music librarians are probably familiar with books such as *Introduction to Music Research* by Ruth Watanabe or *Library Research Guide to Music* by John E. Druesedow Jr. Both are standard, well-written discussions of music research. The latter is a particularly lively and engaging presentation of the material. Such books include many useful concepts for the bibliographic instructor but, like most other music research guides, they are designed for the music specialist. Trying to cover all the resources these books recommend could easily overwhelm a nonmusician at the freshman or sophomore level.

The eager music librarian may be tempted to cover too much material for the sake of completeness. This runs the risk of leaving students in a state of mental dazzle. *Mental dazzle* refers to that confused and blurry-eyed condition a student gets when he or she has been bombarded with so much information, so quickly, that they no longer hear a word the instructor is saying. This commonly occurs during the one-shot instruction sessions when a music faculty member asks the music librarian to cover all the relevant resources in a field of study. The judgment and creativity of the instructor must limit the list of resources he or she plans to present to realistic proportions. He or she should develop a unique repertoire of information resources deemed essential to teach the competencies that will lead the student to information literacy. This is analogous to the writing process where the writer has to decide what not to write so that only the truly essential information is conveyed. Those who fret over being complete and comprehensive may find this process particularly challenging.

A review of various texts for both general and music research techniques finds a common thread with regard to the presentation of information resources.[9] A hierarchical list usually follows the pattern below.

- Library catalog
- Encyclopedias
- Dictionaries
- Bibliographies/discographies, etc.
- Indexes
- Specialized reference works

There is a logical order to this arrangement. Because the library catalog provides access to all the materials in the library it makes sense to start with it. Also, in today's electronic library, the fact that many library catalogs are online reinforces this logic. Since there are so many information resources online, and they utilize many of the same keyboarding and searching skills that the library catalog requires, students are able to transfer many of the competencies learned from the library's online catalog to other online resources. This type of transference is a key component of all teaching/learning models.

Moving down the list the resources become somewhat more specific. For instance, encyclopedias provide the general overview of a topic that is often needed at the start of the research process. They also supply new and unknown terms or concepts relevant to the topic under investigation. These can be defined by a dictionary, which in turn can lead to search terms to use in bibliographies and indexes. This time-tested process takes on greater relevance to students when each resource in the process is examined, evaluated, explored, analyzed, and applied to the student's particular research need.

Timing Is Everything

As essential skills and resources are identified, a key issue emerges. Exactly how much time is available for the instruction of each skill and each resource? It is customary to start by listing the class meeting dates. This is the easy part. Determining how many skills to teach, how much time it will take to teach each skill, and which resources to use, is more difficult. It may become evident that some skills may not be covered, or the time allotted to them will be limited. The instructor must carefully map out a strategy that will address as many information literacy competencies as possible through the use of music information resources in a limited time.

The process of developing these strategies is what Grant Wiggins and Jay McTighe call "backward design." Simply stated, the concept of backward design has three stages. First, start with the "big ideas" or objectives for the class and then work backward to the next stage, assessing how students will demonstrate that they understand the objectives. Once these assessment mechanisms are in place, the instructor should design lectures, demonstrations, and activities that help students achieve success in the assessment. While this may sound simple, it is a practice all too often neglected. Instructors are often too wedded to their time-honored routines to realize their instruction may not be effective in achieving the desired results. Backward design also recognizes that there is never enough time to cover all the content of a subject in detail in a class setting.[10]

When mapping out a course of instruction for multiple class sessions, past experience from teaching single class sessions may not always be helpful. For example, table 1.1 is a list of the resource types taught in a three-credit, semester-long course. The table maps these resource types to their music-specific resources and applications, the competencies they address, and the estimated time it will take to teach, learn, and assess the students' understanding of each resource.

This may seem like a small list of resources for a three-credit course, and the time allotted to teach each type of resource may seem excessive. To achieve information literacy, however, the instructor must remember that it takes more time to learn than to teach. Using the familiar one-shot bibliographic instruction model, the emphasis is on distributing lots of information to the student. The concept of information literacy, on the other hand, focuses on understanding the appropriate application of that information. This is a deeper level of learning that involves practice, refinement, and assessment. This takes much more time, and time must be planned into the teaching schedule. The music librarian should exercise care to ensure the students achieve competence using a resource before moving on to the next one.

An example familiar to most music librarians may help to illustrate this point. Using the one-shot bibliographic instruction model, a music librarian needing to teach music journal indexes may present the *Music Index*, *International Index to Music Periodicals (IIMP)*, *Répertoire International de Littérature Musicale (RILM) Abstracts*, and the *Music Article Guide*, in one fifty-minute period. Given a three-credit course this same librarian may think one class period provides ample time to teach the use of such periodical indexes. But this will not meet the objectives of the information literacy approach. It is not enough to teach students about a skill, or how to use an information tool. Information literacy demands that the student understand when to use a tool and to evaluate the relevance and quality of the information it gathers. This then becomes the objective and, working backward, the

Table 1.1. Time Recommendations for Teaching Information Literacy Competencies

Resource Type	Music-Specific Applications	Competencies Addressed	Recommended No. of Class Sessions (50 min.)
Library Online Catalog	Use Boolean search strategies to locate music materials, both print and media. Students must retrieve material from appropriate collection.	1, 4, 5, 6	3
Encyclopedias	New Grove 2 and Garland Encyclopedia of World Music.	1, 2, 7	2
Dictionaries	New Harvard Dictionary of Music and other specialized dictionaries.	2	1
Indexes	Aggregate full-text databases (e.g., Ebsco, Infotrac), Music Index (print and online), and IIMP.	2, 3	3
Internet Resources	Introduce search engines and browsers to locate music topics. Critically evaluate websites.	1, 4, 5	3
Media Resources	Introduce media as primary source material. Locate and analyze media reviews in the literature. Critically evaluate media used in student's research.	1, 2, 7	2

instructor should design the means for students to demonstrate the creative application of these skills in the research process.

Music librarians whose past experiences come from the one-shot class approach must beware that they do not focus solely on the tool being taught, but rather on the skill or competency that tool is able to develop in the student. Students need to know what a periodical index is, why it is useful, how it can help in finding information, when it is appropriate to use and then demonstrate that they understand and apply this knowledge appropriately. The *Music Index*, *IIMP, RILM Abstracts,* and the *Music Article Guide* are merely tools the students use to demonstrate and practice their competence in dealing with the concept of periodical indexes. If the essential competencies are taught then students can apply them to whichever journal index they encounter.

In the preceding example, a fifty-minute one-shot session would provide little time for the students to demonstrate their understanding and proper application of the information. Using the one-shot model, the instructor can only hope that the deeper understanding of journal indexes will occur during the actual research process and writing of a final paper. When the paper is due, however, students are furiously gathering information to meet a deadline and the thoughtful use of the proper index, introduced weeks prior to the need, does not always occur. There is little time, for example, for students to compare and contrast the *Music Index* and *IIMP* with other periodical indexes or to reinforce and clarify the role of periodical indexes in general. In short, most standard models of bibliographic instruction allow little time for students to demonstrate the state of their information literacy.

Methodology

While a lecture is often necessary to present the basics of most bibliographic instruction, people tend to retain only a portion of what they hear. The average class also contains students with a mix of learning styles. This means the classroom lecture is never enough to reach all students.

Thinking skills and library skills are just that, skills, and as such they require practice. Musicians are well acquainted with the benefits of practice. Years in the practice room are required before stepping on stage to perform. Practice that involves trial, error, correction and more trial is required before the essential musical skills are learned.

Another analogy might be to compare library research skills to athletic skills. A baseball or football team would not be expected to master their skills by taking them into a lecture hall and explaining how to pitch a ball or throw a pass. Nor, would we put them on the field and expect them to perform these skills on the first, second, or even third try. They have to go out in the field and practice the skill over and over.

It is not surprising, therefore, that an occasional guest lecture from the librarian fails to produce information literate students. These single lectures certainly may help students along the way, but it is the wrong model for developing information literacy. When it is understood that these skills take constant practice, correction, and more practice, it becomes clear that the "one-shot" instruction approach falls short. This is the major reason that extended contact time with students is recommended when teaching information literacy.

Having said this, it is also true that not all music librarians have the option to offer a for-credit class in information literacy. While such a course may be optimal, the creative music librarian should find opportunities to maximize contact time and utilize methodologies that imitate those found in for-credit classes.

Assessment

Assessment is the determination of how well, or how poorly, a student is learning a concept or mastering a skill. It must be part of every instructional design. If assessment is not included in the course design, there is no way to determine if the instruction is effective. According to Angelo and Gross there are seven characteristics of classroom assessment.[11] The approach to assessment should be:

1. Learner-centered—assessment focuses both teacher and student on observing and improving learning rather than teaching.
2. Teacher-directed—assessment respects the autonomy of the teacher to determine what to assess and how to assess it.
3. Mutually beneficial—assessment stimulates students by indicating the faculty's interest in their progress and it sharpens faculty's focus on evaluating their effectiveness in teaching.
4. Formative—unlike summative assessments like tests and graded evaluations, formative assessments are rarely graded. They are designed to provide information on how well students are learning and to prepare them for success.
5. Context-specific—assessment should be designed to meet the specific needs of the individual class.
6. Ongoing—since learning is a process, the assessment of that learning must be continual.
7. Rooted in good teaching practice—assessment practice merely systematizes many classroom interactions that good teachers normally encourage.

Almost every interaction with a student then, whether written or spoken, is an opportunity for assessment. When this concept is practiced, the instructor receives continual feedback from the student. Each discussion in class, every student's question, every exercise, every assignment, as well as every quiz and test provides a means to determine what the student thinks about a concept or skill. Therefore, the instructor must plan strategies that make the most of these opportunities. Just as the student must ask the proper questions in their research process, so too must the instructor ask the proper questions to analyze the student's comprehension of the material. In applying a variety of assessment techniques to the library research process, Kuhlthau finds that assessment should provide insight into the students' feelings about the research process. These feelings are influenced by the student's self-awareness of their progress, ability to find focus in their research, time management skills, and the appropriate use of library resources.[12] She recommends tools such as time lines, flow charts, conferences between student and teacher, and writing assignments as information literacy assessment models.

In designing assessment questions, avoid asking leading questions that require a one-word answer. Such short answer questions are quick to produce and even quicker to grade. But these answers provide little to indicate the student's thinking process. Open-ended questions allow the student to describe what they think or understand. Design questions for which students have to describe what they would do to find the answer to a question. Make sure that in any exercise in which a research skill is practiced, the student explains how and why they used the resources they chose. These descriptions are essential to developing critical thinking and assessing information literacy. To assess information literacy, the instructor needs to know how a student thinks through the research process and what steps of logic they make. The final answers a student finds are often not as important as sound reasoning in the research process. If the student's thinking and reasoning are sound, however, the final answers tend to take care of themselves.

Because communication is so essential to assessing information literacy, there must be maximum opportunity for students to provide oral and written feedback in a non-threatening environment. This can occur in writing assignments that Peter Elbow refers to as "low-stakes writing" or free writing. This is writing that receives feedback but not evaluation. Such assignments are not graded for spelling or grammar but are viewed only to discover the student's thoughts about their learning.[13] Whenever teaching nonmusicians, these types of formative assessments are especially useful because they provide a forum that is informative for the instructor but non-judgmental of the student. Non-music students may feel like fish out of water in the music library and anything that puts them at ease will allow them to put their energy into developing the information competencies they need to master.

One means of low-stakes writing are journals in which students record their thoughts about what they are learning. This encourages self-conscious consideration of not only the new skills and concepts but of the learning process itself. Students should be encouraged to provide negative as well as positive feedback regarding lectures, presentations, videos, exercises, readings, etc. This data can be valuable in assessing the effectiveness of both the teaching and learning process. The music librarian teaching nonmusic majors needs this information to determine whether his or her instruction has become too focused on content rather than developing student competence in the information gathering process.

Electronic journals can be an effective method to keep track of student journals efficiently and to help students practice and demonstrate their hardware and software knowledge (general competency 5). Electronic journals are periodic e-mail summaries of what students find new, interesting, useful, confusing, or frustrating in class. These journals need only be about 300 to 500 words long. Electronic journals are not graded but credit is given for each one completed. The electronic format is easy to monitor and cuts down on the instructor's paper shuffle. Some students enjoy sharing their thoughts on the learning process with the instructor while others are more reticent. Instructors may need to turn to creative ways to make the journals part of the grading process to ensure that all students participate in this assessment method in a timely manner. Responding briefly to each student's journal entry lets them know the instructor is personally interested in their progress and encourages regular participation in journal writing. Even though some students may find journals a bother, their assessment value outweighs the student's minor inconvenience.

A Few Thoughts on Technology

During the technology revolution of the past twenty years, the music librarian may have become obsessed with the bells and whistles of technology. Whether teaching students to use the online catalog or to explore the Internet, technology is only a means to an end, not the end itself. Remember that the objective is not to teach the technology, but rather to teach through the technology. As students entering college become more adept at computers, this job has become somewhat easier, but instructors must beware of becoming overconfident in students' knowledge of technology.

If teaching a regularly scheduled class, take a brief inventory of students' computer abilities early in the semester. Inquiries should include the type of equipment the student may have at home or in their dorm, whether they have a modem and an Internet service provider if the school does not provide one, the applications they possess and use regularly, and their familiarity with e-mail as well as the World Wide Web.

To ignore these questions only invites confusion later in the semester when students confess they cannot complete assignments due to a lack of the proper hardware, software, or computer skills. The first two weeks of the semester often finds students struggling to meet technological challenges such as connectivity in the dorms, trouble installing a new modem, discovering their printer is incompatible with the new computer their parents bought them for college, etc. If the music librarian is not a computer specialist, it is wise to find a colleague who is and invite them for a guest visit to class.

In an effort to provide hands-on experience in computer searching, many libraries have developed computer labs designed for library instruction. These are a mixed blessing and all librarians should approach them with caution. While it is advisable for students to have hands-on practice to develop search strategies and online competency, this practice should take place on the instructor's terms. It can be a disaster to place students before computer terminals during a lecture demonstration. Students cannot resist the temptation to conduct independent searches while the librarian is giving instructions. No matter how many times students are asked to stay together and not jump ahead, this is nearly impossible for them to do. Variations in computer speeds, connectivity problems, and student's attention spans provide too many variables during the demonstration and the instructor spends more time keeping everyone connected and on task than on teaching the material.

An effective method to prevent this is to demonstrate technology skills using one projected computer display for the whole class. Make sure a color projector is connected to the computer and in good working order well before the start of class. Demonstrate each computer or online operation for the class and, for in-class practice, individual class members may be called forward to demonstrate their ability in the skill under discussion. Only when this process is complete should students be sent to individual computers. Then the librarian can move from student to student and monitor progress and render aid as needed. If hardware or software problems arise they can be addressed without disturbing the rest of the class. This produces a less stressful and less confusing learning environment for both teacher and student.

Designing Assignments That Facilitate Learning

A key factor in designing assignments is to address the development of both research skills and critical thinking in the same assignment. A recommended approach to achieve this goal is to use facilitated learning. For the purposes of this discussion, facilitated learning refers to any instruction that encourages independent learning. The focus is on participants learning rather than on experts teaching.

Using the facilitated learning model, written exercises provide step-by-step instructions for each learning activity. When the activity is under way, students are asked objective questions to monitor progress. Examples 1 and 2 following demonstrate ways this can be accomplished. Assignments begin with clear instructions to get the student using and examining the tool properly. Then the student is prompted to explore the content of the resource by asking objective questions. Using detailed instructions allows the student to learn on their own, much like a tutorial. This makes the assignment an extension of the class lecture and provides an opportunity to review concepts presented in class. It allows students the opportunity to work at their own pace and practice what they learn. This can also benefit students who are not verbal learners.

In the first example following, the student is asked many questions about the author or editor of the encyclopedia article or volume under consideration. The student is then asked to use this information in a new context, specifically, searching the online catalog, to see what books this author has written. When this information is gathered there are more questions about the topic of these books and their dates of publication. In the end the student is asked to draw conclusions about the information they gathered. This exercise helps the student determine if the writer is an authority on their subject. The reputation of the author or editor should be very obvious to the student by the time they complete the exercise. Yet, many teachers, texts, and handouts tell students to check the authority of a source but never tell the student exactly how to go about determining if someone is an authority. This exercise not only takes students through the process step by step, but also allows them room to think through the process and realize for themselves how easy it is to check on an author's reputation. Students should be encouraged to use a similar process with online journal databases to check on an author's record of journal article publications.

EXAMPLE 1

Music Encyclopedias Assignment

Purpose: To assess students' ability to think critically, examine information resources carefully and accurately, and make appropriate comparisons and contrasts between resources. These skills are among the objectives of this class as stated in the syllabus.

Time to complete: Approximately four hours.

Procedure: Examine related material in two major music encyclopedias. After examining these reference works, specific questions are asked that are designed to help identify strengths and possible weaknesses in each encyclopedia. After answering these questions students are asked to draw some conclusions about what was observed. In evaluating the resource consider the following criteria.

Criteria: Authority, Currency, Bias, Ease of Use, Writing style, Relevance to Topic (usefulness), Special Features.

Grading: 100-point scale.

The two reference works to examine are:

1. *The New Grove Dictionary of Music and Musicians,* 2nd ed. Edited by Stanley Sadie (New York: Grove Dictionaries, Inc.), 2001. (Call number: ML100.N48 2001). This is a 29-volume reference work covering ALL aspects of music. It is available in print and online. It will hereafter be referred to as *NG2*.
2. *Garland Encyclopedia of World Music,* Ruth M. Stone, editor (New York: Garland), 1998. (Call number: ML100.G16 1997). This is a 10-volume work focusing primarily on traditional and popular ethnic music from around the world. This resource is only available in print. Hereafter referred to as *GEWM*.

I. Start by examining the *NG2*. Locate the article on "Africa" and answer the following questions. (Answers are in brackets)
   A. Which volume contains the "Africa" article? [1].
   B. How many pages are devoted to this article? [20].
   C. Following the introductory paragraph of every major article in Groves there is an outline of the article's organization. Identify the major sections in the article on Africa.
      1. [Ethnic groups, Languages and style areas]
      2. [Historical sources and research history]
      3. [Musical structures and cognition]
         a. [General]
         b. [Principles of timing]
         c. [Time-line patterns]
         d. [Tonal systems]
         e. [Multipart singing, instrumental polyphony and illusory effects]
      4. [Music and society]
      5. [Modern developments]

D. Does this article have a bibliography? Yes [X] No ___
E. Does this article contain music examples? Yes [X] No ___
F. Does this article provide a list of African music recordings? Yes [X] No ___
G. Does this article provide a list of videos on African music? Yes ___ No [X]
H. Does this article contain pictures? Yes [X] No ___
I. Who wrote this article on Africa? [Gerhard Kubik]
J. Using the Library's online catalog, conduct a name (author) search for this author. How many books does the library have that he or she has written in whole or in part? [Nine]
K. After scanning the list of books by this author, found in the online catalog, what topic or topics does he or she generally write about? [African music] (Hint: if a work is in a foreign language try looking at the subject headings to determine the content.)
L. From examining the copyright dates of the books written by this author, how many years has he or she been writing on this topic? [Thirty-one years]

II. Examine the *GEWM*. A major difference in this Encyclopedia is that instead of one article on music in Africa, there is an entire volume devoted to the subject (volume 1). Turn to page ix in this volume that has the heading "About the Garland Encyclopedia of World Music." Read this section carefully.
  A. What are the three major sections found in each volume of this Encyclopedia?
    1. [Introduction to the region]
    2. [Issues and Processes that link music to the region]
    3. [Detailed accounts of individual music cultures]

Turn to page xii. Read the section marked "How this volume is organized." Using the material presented in this section answer the following questions:
  B. Does this encyclopedia have articles arranged alphabetically? Yes ___ No [X]
  C. What major geographical feature of Africa was often used to divide the country for purposes of study, but which the editors of this Encyclopedia choose not to use? [Sahara Desert]
  D. According to this article, the *GEWM* provides which four (4) research tools? [Maps, Cross-references, Bibliography, Illustrations].

E. Does this encyclopedia provide maps? Yes [X] No ___
F. Does this encyclopedia provide pictures? Yes [X] No ___
G. Does this encyclopedia provide bibliographies? Yes [X] No ___
H. Does this encyclopedia provide a list of videos on African music? Yes [X] No ___
I. There is an African instrument called an *Mbira*, also known as a "thumb piano." It is a plucked idiophone and, according to the *NG2*, it is classified as a lamellophone. Using the index in the back of the *GEWM* vol. 1, try to locate an article or articles on this instrument.
J. Now, check the glossary for the same information. Is there an entry for *Mbira* or lamellophone that directs you to page references for articles about these instruments? Yes [X] No ___
K. Turning back to the table of contents in the Africa volume of the *GEWM*, try to locate any articles by the author of the *NG2* article on Africa (see I. j above), and if so how many? Yes [X], I found [2] articles. No ___, there were no articles by this author.
L. Who is the editor of volume one of the *GEWM*? [Ruth Stone]
M. Using the online catalog, search for the name of this editor. How many books by this author does the library have? [5]
N. What topic or topics does this author write about? [African Music and Culture]
O. From examining the copyright dates of the books written by this author how many years has he or she been writing on this topic? [Twenty-seven years]

III. Writing assignment: Use the following criteria to evaluate the encyclopedias: Authority, Currency, Ease of Use, Clarity of Writing, Bias. For each criterion be sure to provide a discussion for both the *NG2* and the *GEWM*. Include examples to support your observations.

In a final paragraph, state which encyclopedia you prefer and why. The entire written portion of this assignment should be at least 1000-1500 words or approximately two to three pages long.

EXAMPLE 2

Website Evaluation Assignment

Purpose: This project will help students expand their knowledge of the world music topic they are investigating while also demonstrating their ability to evaluate critically the online information they find.

Estimated time to complete: Two to three hours.

Procedure: Conduct a web search using the world music topic you have selected. Be sure to consider various searching techniques including Boolean searches, truncation, proximity searching, and the appropriate use of browsing and keyword searches.

1. Please indicate the specific world music topic under investigation:

   Conduct a World Wide Web search to locate two (2) websites that relate to your topic.
2. Which directories or search engines did you use to locate relevant websites?

3. Indicate the exact search term(s) used to locate these sites and any special commands or search functions used:

4. Provide the URLs for the two sites that you will discuss:

5. Use the criteria below to evaluate critically the sites examined. Review the sites carefully, look at different pages in the site, examine links, etc. Take notes along the way.

When your investigation is complete, write a three page essay that provides an evaluation of the two sites you examined. Be sure to address each of the criteria below in the discussion. In a final paragraph, give an overall recommendation of the two websites. Indicate which seems superior.

Criteria

    Authority: Is the author identified and, if so, well regarded? Is there a biography? Are you led to additional information about the author?
    Bias: Is it clear what organization is sponsoring the page? Is there a link to the sponsoring organization's website? Is the page actually an ad disguised as information?
    Citations: Does the author provide sources or a bibliography?
    Dates: Credible sites should list the date of creation. When was the last update?

Efficiency: Does the site load fast? Is it available at different times of the day? Is it bogged down with graphics?

Context: Is the information presented in context? Did you check out the "top" of the site or "Home" to see what the context of the site is?

Graphics: Are the graphics used to make a point? Is that point clear? Are graphics used to make the site look "cool" and really just increase the time needed to paint the screen?

Misinformation: Does the site contain opinion verbs and appeal to emotions rather than fact? Is there information that conflicts with what you already know about the subject?

Navigability: Is it easy to get around the site? Links should be easy to identify and grouped in some logical order. Organization should be readily apparent.

Pertinent (Useful): Does this site really address your informational need? If not, move on to a more useful site.

Quantity of Information: How much material does the site provide? Some sites are added to regularly so several visits may be needed. Does the site provide the breadth of information you need?

General Comments: Overall, how satisfied are you with your visit to the website? Did it expand your knowledge of the subject? Did it address some or all of the questions you have about the topic? If so, which specific questions were answered by this site?

The simple and straightforward objective portions of the assignments above can build a student's self-confidence. This is stated in the list of competencies as one of the affective qualities librarians seek to foster in students. Students who experience success early in the exercise will be more motivated to continue working on the more difficult sections, such as the essay questions, which are subjective and require critical thinking and analysis. Also, the objective questions quickly assess the student's basic information skills. If the student is having difficulty with the basic functions of the tool, the objective questions can isolate the area that needs the instructor's attention. Asking only essay questions may not reveal specific areas of misunderstanding in using the information resource. Remember, the objective section of the exercise is only able to assess what the student does, not what he or she thinks. This process is important, however, in bringing the class to a common level of experience before asking questions about what the students understand. This section is also the easiest for the instructor to correct and grade.

Critical Thinking

After completing the objective portion of their assignment, students must be asked to find meaning in what was observed and reveal some of the thought processes that lie behind their actions. This may take the form of comparing and contrasting, evaluating, and finding potential applications for the tools or skills learned. This reflective portion of the assignment requires higher-level critical thinking. It is a good place for students to externalize their thinking process and demonstrate their understanding of the main concepts. Feedback may be oral or written. Information gleaned from the subjective questions is invaluable in assessing a student's progress toward information literacy. The ability of the instructor to analyze the thought process of the student is a factor that tutorials are not always able to evaluate because they are usually designed for objective rather than subjective responses. The subjective portion of the assignment also provides another opportunity for students to practice their writing or speaking skills. The instructor must also provide adequate feedback to correct faulty logic or misunderstandings. The major drawback to these subjective questions, if they are written responses, is that they require more time for the instructor to review and correct.

Online Tutorials

An alternative method of presenting facilitated learning is the use of online tutorials. The ambitious instructor may wish to create their own online tutorial, but this will require a fair amount of preparation and computer expertise. For the instructor with neither time nor technical expertise there are products that provide templates that simplify the process of creating instructional assignments on the Internet. Web products designed for educators such as WebCT or Blackboard are excellent for this purpose. Many colleges and universities make such products available to their faculty to create web environments that augment classroom instruction. By using web-based exercises, an instructor can create quizzes that test a student's knowledge of particular resources. These usually take the form of multiple-choice questions. Each response can be accompanied by an explanation that aids the learner in understanding why they may have chosen the answer they did.

Since online tutorials can be a major undertaking, they may not be an option for the librarian with a busy teaching schedule. There are, however, a number of good tutorials available for free on the Internet. These usually treat general library resources and can augment the music resources presented by the music librarian. Some of these tutorials include:

http://tilt.lib.utsystem.edu/
http://www.hawaii.edu/infoliteracy/
http://www.library.unlv.edu/help/tutorial/
http://library.ndnu.edu/tutorial.htm

For tutorials dealing with the use of Internet resources the following sites are useful.

http://libweb.hawaii.edu/uhmlib/internet/internet_guides.html
http://www.library.cornell.edu/okuref/search.html
http://lib.nmsu.edu/instruction/eval.html

Allie Goudy at Western Illinois University has developed a site designed specifically for music research skills. It provides an excellent introduction to music information resources using an information literacy approach. This site can be used as a model or parts of it may be incorporated into assignments. The site is located at:

http://www.wiu.edu/library/units/music/tutorial/main254.htm

For more examples of library instruction tutorials, along with practical instructions on how to develop such sites, consult Susan Smith's book *Web-Based Instruction: A Guide for Libraries*, which is listed in the further reading section at the end of this chapter. An excellent online resource for links to educational websites including tutorials is www.merlot.org. Merlot stands for Multimedia Education Resource for Learning and Online Teaching, and all the sites it lists are peer reviewed.

Games

Games can be wonderful learning tools. They can be used to review material, practice skills, and break up the tedium if a unit is particularly long and challenging. Games also help build a good rapport between students and teacher. With a little imagination almost any game that requires questions and answers can be adapted to classroom use. Here are a few that can be particularly useful.

Bluff and Bluster

This simple dictionary game has gained popularity due to its commercialization by one of the major toy companies. It is especially useful as a learning tool after teaching a unit on dictionaries. In the unit the instructor should examine various music and nonmusic dictionaries, and list the various elements a good dictionary entry may contain such as pronunciation, classification, etymology, definition, usage, etc. This knowledge is useful for students in any field of study. The game provides a fun and enjoyable opportunity for students to conceptualize the elements of a dictionary entry by making up convincing definitions to unfamiliar words.

Object of the game: To invent a definition for each word in play that could be mistaken by the other players as the correct definition and/or to identify the correct definition for each word in play.

Preparation for play: This game requires:

- A stack of 3 × 5 cards or notepaper for each player.

- Pen or pencils for each player.
- A stack of 3 × 5 word cards prepared in advance. These are uncommon words drawn from a variety of dictionaries, including music dictionaries. Copy the word on one side of the card and its definition on the reverse.
- A die or pair of dice.

Playing the game:

1. Pass out a small stack of 3 × 5 cards or notepaper and a pencil to each player.
2. Use the die or dice (depending on the size of the class) to roll to see who will go first. Using two dice in a large class cuts down on the chances of a tie. The high roller becomes the leader and is the first to read the definition for the other players.
3. The leader starts by taking a word card from the stack. He reads only the word and spells it for the other players. Each player writes the word on one of his or her cards or pieces of notepaper.
4. Each player then invents a meaning to the word that will bluff the other players and writes it on their card.
5. Each player then puts his or her name on the card and all the cards are collected.
6. The leader reviews all the entries making sure he or she can read them convincingly. After making sure they are in random order he or she reads each definition aloud including the correct definition the leader has. The definitions should be read a second time so players can decide which they think is the true definition.
7. Moving clockwise from the leader, go around the room and allow each player to vote for the definition he or she thinks is the correct one. As each vote is cast the leader jots down the initials of the voter on the card with the definition they voted for.

8. Once all votes are cast the leader reveals the true meaning of the word and tallies the scores.
9. The player to the left of the leader becomes the new leader and play continues in like manner.

Scoring:

- One point is awarded for each successful bluff. For example, if a player's definition fooled three other players into choosing it as a correct definition that player is awarded three points.
- Two points are given to each player who chooses the true meaning.
- Two points are given to the leader if no one chooses the true meaning of the word.
- Three points are given to any player who submits a definition that is similar or very close to the correct meaning.

Players submitting correct definitions: While this is essentially a bluffing game, there is a reward for submitting a correct definition. If the leader receives such an entry it should be set aside and the player that submitted it automatically receives three points and is prevented from voting in the round. Other than this exception, the round is played normally. If the leader should receive two or more correct, or nearly correct definitions, the round is cancelled and a new word is drawn.

How to win: The player with the highest score wins. The end of game should occur when all the players have had a chance to be the leader. In a large class, teams can be formed and students can work together to come up with convincing bluffs.

While students are having a good time with this game, they learn some useful lessons. If they are clever and hope to fool the other players they will find that their fake definitions need to emulate the elements of a good dictionary entry. Students are often creative, assigning parts of speech, fake etymologies, and imaginative definitions to their terms. Having small prizes for the winners adds to the fun of the competition.

Words drawn from music dictionaries that have been used with good success include: Embolada (a type of Brazilian folk singing using alliteration and onomatopoeias sung very fast), Ophicleide (large nineteenth-century brass instrument with keys and holes on its sides that was a precursor to the tuba), and Acciaccatura (Italian name for an ornament in keyboard music).

Scavenger Hunt

This game employs any number of print or online information resources. It assesses the student's efficiency in conducting research and assesses a variety of information literacy competencies. The game consists of creating sets of questions that can be answered using specific information tools in the music library. The trick of the game is that the students work against the clock. This tests their ability to analyze questions and use the appropriate tools to answer them efficiently. The game atmosphere created by choosing teams, and awarding prizes rather than grades, replaces the stress of the timed environment with a bit of fun.

Object of the game: To answer a set of questions in the best way and in the shortest time possible.

Preparation for play:

1. Before class, prepare sets of music-related questions that make use of resources that have been discussed in class. Each team will need to answer the same number of questions. At least three questions are recommended but more can be added depending on difficulty. Use care in developing the questions to make sure each team has different questions and that a variety of information resources are used. If each team has the same questions, they will be vying for the same resources and that complicates the game. Sample questions are provided below.

2. At the start of class, divide the class into two or more teams. Each team gets its own set of questions.
3. Teams may elect a captain or the instructor may appoint one. The captain should help determine who will answer each question, motivate the team, and make sure they return to class on time.
4. When the instructor says go, each team has thirty minutes to find the answer to all the questions and provide an explanation as to how the information was found.
5. Players may not ask for help from a library staff member.

Scoring:

- For each correct answer the team gets one point.
- The team gets one point for using an appropriate information tool irrespective of finding the correct answer.
- Teams loose a point for each incorrect answer.
- Two bonus points are awarded to the team that gets all their team members back in the classroom first. This is an incentive to work efficiently and keep all teams on task.

How to win: The team with the highest score wins. The scoring is designed to reward speed, efficiency, accuracy, and sound judgment.

In this game, students who do not apply critical thinking in determining the best research tool to use fall behind quickly. Even with each team member dealing with one question, some questions still may go unanswered. This can be very revealing for the students. Some who consider themselves quite sophisticated researchers may find that when they need to work with a deadline (in this case only thirty minutes) they have difficulty. Make sure there is an opportunity to repeat this game later in the semester so students may gauge their improvement.

A variation on this game can even be used when the instructor is out of town. Instead of canceling class, prepare a set of questions for each student and leave the questions in an envelope with the student's name on it at a public service counter in the library. During class time, the students can come to the counter and pick up their envelope. A time and date stamp may be used to monitor the time the students worked on the questions. Just as in the game played in class, points are divided between the correct answer to the question and the method used to find the answer.

Rewarding students for explaining how they found their answers provides another means of assessment. Students sometimes find the correct answers in unusual ways. Occasionally, a student stumbles upon the answer by pure accident in a most unlikely place. Points should be awarded for any answer that demonstrates sound logic, i.e. any method that, when repeated, has a good chance of yielding positive results. This can be used as a teaching opportunity to illustrate the unreliability of using the improper resources (or just dumb luck!). The important thing is to make sure students understand the value of using resources that yield consistently correct results. Students who stumble upon the correct answer always get a point. Those who use reliable and efficient methods earn an extra point. Notice that the instructions and questions below facilitate learning by providing helpful hints and clues that can aid students in working independently.

Scavenger Hunt questions:
Instructions: The questions below can be answered using print and electronic resources that are accessible in the library. Each resource has been discussed in class. Do not ask the person at the reference desk for extensive help. To answer all the questions in the time allotted be prepared to apply a few practical research skills. These include:

- A. Think through the question to determine what is being asked. Do you need information about people, places, things, or ideas? Does the question require the information to come from a book, a journal, or a website?

B. Determine the most efficient tool to use to find the answer. Some questions require that you look in an index. The index you need may be online or in print, it may be general or music specific. This is usually the case when asked for a journal article or a review. Remember, a library catalog is a great place to look for books or media, or to see if the library owns a journal title, but it is NOT the place to find the contents of a journal. Be sure to use the proper tool to find the information most efficiently.

Here are the questions.

1. In what year did Billy Joel release his album *Piano Man*? What resource was used to locate this information?
   Answer: 1973. The answer can be found in most music biographical reference resources. *Baker's Biographical Dictionary of Music and Musicians* or *Current Musicians* both provide the answer. A monographic biography of Billy Joel or an Internet search will also work but may take more time to track down and verify the answer.
2. There is an article about the jazz performer Stan Getz that discusses his winning a Grammy award in 1963. The author of the article is L. Feather. Provide the full bibliographic citation for this article. What resource was used to locate this information?
   Answer: L. Feather "Jazz Samba: the Other Side of the Record" *Down Beat* 30 (August 29, 1963): 12–13.

In this instance a journal index is clearly required. *Music Index* is the obvious choice (to a music librarian but not so for many undergraduates). The 1963 date is the tip off to steer clear of the online version and head straight for the print version of *Music Index* because currently the online version only goes back to 1979. A parenthetical mention of the Grammy award in the citation lets the student know this is the correct citation instead of another article about Getz also by Feather.

3. Locate a compact disc that contains the song "Hodie Christus natus est." Explain exactly how this information was located. From what was presented in the bibliographic record, what type of music is this song?
Answer: The answer will vary depending on the library setting in which the game is played. Any CD containing a title in a foreign language will suffice provided the subject headings reveal the nature of the contents of the CD.

In this example the vocal work can be located by searching the title as a phrase using a keyword search in the library's online catalog. The search should be limited to locate only sound recordings. Scanning the results of such a search reveals that there are various vocal works on this text but that they are all sacred works and deal with Christmas.

In this exercise the students should locate the call number of a specific compact disc and limit their search by format and title in the contents field. The point is to have the students use the online catalog effectively and get used to reading the bibliographic record for as much useful data as possible. In this case, the subject heading reveals the type of music in question. Mastery of Latin is not required.

4. A friend tells you that you should read the article "Madonna Goes to Camp" that he read in the early 1990s. He can't remember anything else about this article. Exactly where is this article located? Where did you find this information? Why did you select this resource?
Answer: Corliss, Richard. "Madonna Goes to Camp." *Time* 142, issue 17 (October 25, 1993): 73.

This question provides an excellent opportunity for students to learn that music research is not confined to music resources. Note that there is no indication in the question that this information is in a music journal or magazine. Because of the popular nature of the topic students should consult a general journal index as well as music specific indexes. In this instance, resources such as the *Readers Guide to Periodic Literature*, Ebscohost's *Academic Search Premier*, or Gale's *Expanded Academic Index* (a.k.a. *Infotrac*) will work nicely. *Music Index* and *The International Index to Music Periodicals* will not work because they do not index nonmusic journals such as Time, despite the fact that such journals often contain valuable information on music.

Keyword searching in an electronic database is the most efficient approach to this question. A print index will work too but, because the date is not specific (and people's memories are notoriously unreliable), several volumes must be checked to find the answer.

SUMMARY

- Music information resources provide an excellent means for teaching information literacy if the proper learning context is provided. The key to success is not simply teaching the mechanics of using music resources but rather teaching the information literacy concepts that apply to all information resources.
- Building upon well-formulated information literacy competencies helps instructors focus on core objectives.
- Linking library skills with course- or assignment-related content is one of the best ways to teach information literacy. This linkage makes practicing the required skills relevant to the student and increases motivation and retention.
- Developing an effective syllabus can aid in identifying clear objectives, organizing materials, identifying essential resources, and managing time for instruction.
- Use "backward planning" to plan enough time for instruction that is focused on the big ideas and ensure that core competencies are assessed appropriately.
- Be passionate about the instructional objectives.

- Learning takes more time than teaching. Proper information literacy instruction requires more time than is available in the customary one-shot bibliographic instruction session.
- Assessment is an essential component of all instructional designs. Continual, ongoing assessment benefits both teacher and learner.
- Technology is only a means to an end. The focus must always be on developing information literacy. Learning computer skills is only a means to that end, not the end itself.
- Use facilitated learning that creates independent learning when designing assignments. Facilitated learning means providing clear, step-by-step instructions, making learning active, and asking for feedback that assesses understanding.
- Games can provide a fun, creative and enjoyable means to practice skills and assess information literacy.

NOTES

1. LaGuardia, Cheryl, et al., *Teaching the New Library: A How-to-do-it Manual for Planning and Designing Instructional Programs* (New York: Neal Schuman Pub., 1996), 3–6.

2. The experiences that comprise this discussion took place over a six-year period from 1996 to 2002 at the University of Hawaii at Manoa. The University of Hawaii is a postsecondary education system composed of 10 campuses throughout the island state. The flagship research institution is the University of Hawaii at Manoa (UHM), which began in 1907 as a land-grant college of agriculture and mechanic arts. The campus currently is the home to 17,000 students enrolled in 88 bachelor, 87 masters, and 55 doctoral degree programs. About 70 percent of the students are undergraduates, 55 percent are women, and 72 percent attend full time. The mean age of students is 26. The music department is part of the College of Arts and Humanities and offers a Bachelor of Arts, Bachelor of Music, and Bachelor of Education in music. At the graduate level the department offers masters degrees in ethnomusicology, music education, composition, performance, musicology and theory and the Ph.D. is offered in composition, ethnomusicology, musicology, and music education.

3. Association of College and Research Libraries, "Standards and Guidelines," Information Literacy 2003, http://www.ala.org/Content/NavigationMenu/ACRL/Issues_and_Advocacy1/Information_Literacy1/Information_Literacy.htm (16 September 2003).

4. Jean Key Gates, *Guide to the Use of Libraries and Information Sources* (New York: McGraw-Hill, 1994), 75–92.

5. Nancy Thomas Totten, "Teaching Students to Evaluate Information: A Justification," *RQ* 29, no. 3 (Spring 1990): 348.

6. Diane Nahl and Violet Harada, "Composing Boolean Search Statements: Self-Confidence, Concept Analysis, Search Logic, and Error," *School Library Media Quarterly* 24, no. 4 (Summer 1996): 200.

7. Carolyn Collier Kuhlthau, *Seeking Meaning: A Process Approach to Library and Information Service* (Norwood, N.J.: Ablex, 1993), 42–53.

8. For an alternative list of qualities an information literate student should possess see Debbie Orr and Margie Wallin, "Information Literacy and Flexible Delivery: Are We Meeting the Student Needs?" *Australian Academic & Research Libraries* 32, no. 3 (September 2001): 195.

9. Music research guides following this formula include: Ruth T. Watanabe, *Introduction to Music Research* (Englewood Cliffs, N.J.: Prentice-Hall, 1967); Dominique-René De Lerma, *Involvement with Music: Resources for Music Research* (New York: Harper's College Press, 1976); and John E. Druesedow, *Library Research Guide to Music: Illustrated Search Strategy and Sources* (Ann Arbor, Mich.: Pierian Press, 1982). The text used in LIS 100, which follows the same presentation of material, is Jean Key Gates, *Guide to the Use of Libraries and Information Sources* (New York: McGraw-Hill, 1994).

10. Grant Wiggins and Jay McTighe, *Understanding by Design* (Alexandria, Va.: Association for Supervision and Curriculum Development, 1998), 7–19.

11. Thomas A. Angelo and K. Patricia Cross, *Classroom Assessment Techniques: A Handbook for College Teachers*, 2nd ed. (San Francisco: Jossey-Bass, 1993), 4–7.

12. Carol Collier Kuhlthau, *Teaching the Library Research Process*, 2nd ed. (Metuchen, N.J.: Scarecrow, 1994), 172–178.

13. *Peter Elbow on Writing*, produced & conceptualized by Patricia H. Mangan; directed by Sut Jhally (Media Education Foundation, 1995), videocassette, 43 min.

2

Teaching the Graduate Music Research Course

Laura M. Snyder

INTRODUCTION

Whether it is called *Music Bibliography*, *Introduction to Musicology*, or something similar, some type of music research course is often required in graduate degree programs in music. Such courses are usually expected to cover a broad spectrum of reference tools, research methods and sources, and the mechanics of the scholarly apparatus, as they apply to music. While such courses have traditionally been a curriculum requirement for graduate programs in musicology and music theory, many music programs now also include such a requirement for advanced performance degrees.[1]

In the traditional approach to teaching music bibliography, the instructor often attempts to cover as many reference sources as possible, within an organized structure. The students are required to complete a substantial research paper in addition to numerous smaller assignments, quizzes, and the like. This is a rigorous endeavor for student and teacher alike, and often frustrating to teach, because many students become overwhelmed by the volume of material, and are often lacking in motivation to do more than simply get through the course with an acceptable grade. Clearly, many students find this type of course neither relevant to their needs as performers nor engaging to their curiosity. Furthermore, even the students who do well in the course later seem to forget much of what they have learned.

One solution is to decrease the number of sources covered, and instead to concentrate more on depth of coverage and quality of learning. This may help to some extent, although while students learn to use the standard music reference sources somewhat better, many are still mystified by the research and writing process, and often remain unconvinced that music research skills will be useful to them as performers.

The challenge in teaching a music bibliography and research course is to make the research process come alive for students. The course should be based on the interweaving of three basic learning objectives: to understand the process of research, especially as manifested in the field of music; to learn to make effective use of research sources and tools in the field of music; and to understand and correctly demonstrate the mechanics of a good research paper. Appendix A lists general course information and Appendix B provides an example of a basic schedule that can be used in a one-semester course to weave the three strands together.

THE COURSE PAPER

The three basic learning objectives listed above are all integrally connected in the central project of this course, a research paper. There are, of course, many possible topics for successful use in such a course. A project focusing on one musical work or an identifiable group of works by a single composer allows the performance-oriented students to research topics that may directly complement and support their applied music studies. An example of this assignment may be found in Appendix C. While a more structured research project—limiting the topic choice to certain composers' works or particular avenues of investigation—may provide greater control over the assignment, many students at this level will appreciate a broader choice of topics. Success in this course is highest when the student becomes truly engaged in the research process, and this is most likely to happen when there is a strong interest in the topic chosen for the paper. Moreover, students who have not done a major research paper before can carry out the process with more confidence if they begin with a topic that is familiar, even if from a very different perspective.

In this course, the students work on their papers for the entire semester, turning in preliminary work along the way. While not every assignment or class activity can be designed to feed directly into this research process, many can be related to the paper in some way. For example, in an early assignment on searching the library catalog, students explore the availability of books, scores, and recordings related to their chosen topic, a first step for preparation of their topic proposals. The paper preparation assignments help to ensure that the students do not put off starting their research until the last few weeks of the semester, and also allow the teacher to see their work in various stages. This provides a richer, more active learning experience, and can help to deter plagiarism. Many students have admitted that this was the first time they did a *real* research paper, rather than putting something together at the last minute. For this "building block" approach to be successful, however, the teacher must be committed to grading and returning the preliminary assignments in a timely manner, so that the students have the necessary feedback before tackling the next step in their research. Having the students discuss their research in class at various points during the semester is also tremendously valuable. Students are often reluctant to do this, but they can learn a lot from each other, especially when they are willing to divulge the problems and frustrations they have encountered.

Research is not a linear process, nor does it follow the same predictable pattern for every student or for every research project. "Doing research carefully and reporting it clearly are hard work. However carefully you plan, research follows a crooked path, taking unexpected turns, even looping back on itself."[2] Obviously, this reality conflicts with a teacher's natural desire to have specific tasks accomplished by certain dates, not to mention a student's tendency to want closure and a good grade with each interim assignment that is turned in. Be clear with students at the outset that the research process is not always a predictable one, and that assignments sometimes need to be a little contrived so that students can demonstrate their understanding of concepts that may not apply to a given research project.

In the plan outlined in Appendix C, the three Paper Preparation Assignments provide interim goals to help guide the students through the research process, while providing some flexibility for the vagaries of the endeavor. Each assignment, in a different way, ties together all three of the basic learning objectives of the course.

In Paper Preparation Assignment no. 1, the students prepare preliminary literature bibliographies on their topics. "Preliminary" needs to be emphasized to the students, as they cannot determine at this stage what sources will really be useful for the papers they will turn in at the end of the semester. For this assignment, some rather contrived requirements for content are added to make sure that the students have located, and can properly cite, a variety of materials.

Paper Preparation Assignment no. 2 can sometimes seem very artificial, especially for the students who are not yet at the point of writing their papers. This assignment does, however, teach some crucial lessons, and helps students get started in the writing process.

Paper Preparation Assignment no. 3 can be especially challenging for teacher and student alike, because at this stage it becomes most apparent that research is not a linear process, and that each student must find his or her own way through the drafting stage to the final product. Providing multiple options in this assignment helps to accommodate the students' various working styles. For students who are inexperienced in the writing of research papers, the best results generally happen when students turn in the complete paper, or at least a significant portion, in draft form for initial review and comments. This works even better when the teacher meets with the student to talk about the process. Though a heavy time commitment for the teacher, this practice results in a final paper that is more pleasurable to read and easier to grade. Even without this kind of individualized attention at the draft stage, however, many students will achieve something new with Preparation Assignment no. 3, simply by gathering their thoughts and beginning the writing process well ahead of the due date for the final paper rather than waiting until the last minute.

While much emphasis in the course is placed upon the research paper as the traditional proof of scholarship, performance need not be left entirely out of the picture. At the end of the semester, students discuss their papers briefly in class, and are encouraged to include a performance when feasible. Some students who are not particularly adept at writing are much better at conveying the results of their research through these miniature lecture recitals.

The First Strand: The Process of Research

Unless the participants have a clear understanding and appreciation for the research process, a music bibliography course risks becoming a dull recitation of endless facts about sources and their proper citation. Ideally, a graduate student should have already gained some experience in scholarly research before this point. Sadly, this is often not the case, but a little course time spent on providing a theoretical framework is well worth the effort. A well-chosen textbook on the subject can provide tremendous support for this strand of the course.[3] Any such text should not just be assigned reading, but should be discussed in class and augmented with examples applied specifically to music research.

What Is Research?

Many students come into this course lacking a clear understanding of what research is, or how it might apply to their own lives and careers as musicians. The prospect of writing a "real" research paper over a period of weeks and months is often foreign, and sometimes frightening. The first step in this thread of the course, then, is to explore the concept of research, to help the students understand that research can take many different guises to serve a multitude of purposes.[4] The description of research as engagement in a conversation that takes place over decades, or even centuries, helps to elucidate the writing process, but also makes sense in the context of performance.[5] The relationship between writer and reader seems to have more meaning for many music students when an analogy is drawn to the relationship between performer and listener. It is important at this first stage for the students to begin to understand the concept of "audience" as it applies to writing, and to appreciate the difference between writing for other scholars and writing for general readers.[6] This is also helpful in explaining why CD liner notes, program notes, and many Internet sites, however skillfully prepared, may not be appropriate sources on which to base a research paper.

Students also need to understand music research as a unique complex of historical conversations. A reading assignment and class discussion on the articles about musicology in *The New Grove*, and the *New Harvard Dictionary* provide a good introduction, and also set the stage for later discussion of the sources and tools of music research, the second strand of the course.[7, 8]

Selecting a Topic

As prescribed in Appendix C, students benefit by turning in a paper topic proposal very early in the semester. This may present some difficulties for them, but they are usually better served in the long run if they can at least focus their attention on a particular composer and work that interests them as they begin to explore the various research sources. The requirement to formulate a topic, question, and rationale for their papers is necessarily artificial at this point. It is important for them to begin thinking along these lines, but also to be reassured that they may (and most cases will need to) change the focus of their respective papers as they progress through the research process. They should be discouraged from changing to a different composer and work altogether after this point, however.

The Research Argument

For many students, the most difficult aspect of writing a good research paper is formulating a good research argument or thesis.[9] This is also the most crucial step in encouraging them to move beyond the all-too-common practice of stringing together pieces of information, often taken out of context, and with little thought about what they are really trying to prove. To see the principles of a research argument at work, the class should read and discuss an assigned research article in music that demonstrates these principles. An example that works particularly well for this is the article by William S. Newman on the opening trill in Beethoven's Opus 96.[10] It is relatively short, and focuses on one particular performance question. Students are often amazed at first that an entire article could be written on one little trill. This in itself is instructive to students who are all too accustomed to thinking of research papers as exercises in gathering as much "stuff" as possible to fill the required number of pages. Many students at this stage need to be encouraged to narrow the focus of their papers, and to concentrate on building a convincing argument supported by more in-depth research than they have done in the past. The Newman article presents an interesting and somewhat challenging example with which to discuss the components that make up a research argument. As Newman makes very clear, since there are no primary sources to support his argument, his case is built on circumstantial evidence, and therefore his writing style makes abundant use of what Booth, Colomb, and Williams would describe as qualifications that acknowledge the limits of his claims. Some students, in fairly lively class discussions, have expressed little patience with Newman's use of these "weasel words" at first, until they come to understand the reasons for his use of this kind of language in this particular instance. One of the most difficult of the "argument" concepts for students to grasp is that of warrants.[11] Here, the Newman article presents an interesting challenge, because it is difficult to find a good example of an explicit warrant. As is typical of many writings aimed at other scholars in music, this article seems to rely on assumed warrants. This concept begins to make more sense to students, however, when we identify those assumed warrants, and discuss the reasons that they are left unstated by the author.

The Newman article is just one of many possible choices for this reading assignment. Several articles from the collection *The Creative Process* have also been used.[12] The article by Steven Ledbetter on Gilbert and Sullivan's *Trial by Jury* works especially well for this purpose.[13]

The Second Strand: Sources and Tools in Music

The second strand of the course, and the most central part of the content, focuses on the sources and tools that are used in music research. There are many different ways to organize this material. One practical approach is a division into three sections: library catalogs, literature about music, and editions of music. The order in which these three sections are taught has a strong connection to the way in which students are encouraged to go about their research.

Library Catalogs

The library catalog, in whatever form it may take, is the most basic tool for locating materials in a library. Before the students can progress very far with a research project, they must have enough facility with the library's catalog to be able to use it effectively to determine what basic sources are available on their chosen topic, such as scores and recordings of the work they will be investigating, and books about the composer. While most graduate students already have some familiarity with using a library catalog, many do not know how to search a catalog effectively, especially for finding music materials. With the many different online catalog interfaces now available, the details of how to approach this will vary with the individual library setting, but even with the availability of fairly sophisticated keyword searching capabilities, an understanding of concepts such as uniform titles, consistent name headings, and Library of Congress Subject Headings is still essential for truly effective music searches. These are not easy concepts to explain to students, and it is important to remember that the goal of this course is not to turn them into music catalogers. Most students, however, are able to achieve at least a basic understanding of these concepts, and how they can be used to make a catalog search more effective. This knowledge is further reinforced later in the course, when they discover how these same principles work (or sometimes do not work) in electronic databases. Lessons learned for effective keyword searching of a library catalog, such as the use of Boolean operators and truncation symbols, will also serve the students well as they explore other electronic tools later in the semester.

Literature About Music

As will be seen in the "Basic Schedule" (Appendix B), a large portion of the course is devoted to the study of literature about music, including dictionaries and encyclopedias, composer bibliographies and thematic catalogs, books and dissertations, periodicals and the indexing and abstracting tools to access their content, literature on performance practice and notation, discography, and subject/genre bibliographies. The exact content will vary according to availability of resources in the library at hand, and also according to the interests and needs of the students.

The order in which these various types of sources are studied in the course is very much tied to the order in which students might logically go about gathering the information they need for their research. First, begin with encyclopedias and dictionaries to gain an overview of the topic, define appropriate terminology, and identify key sources through bibliographies. Next, look for relevant books, for a more indepth overview and more extensive bibliographies. The published bibliographies devoted to single composers can be extremely helpful at this point, and it does not hurt to begin introducing the concept of the Thematic Catalog, though it will be discussed in more depth later in the course. Research at the journal article level is the most fruitful stage for many topics, and also the most difficult for the students, as many of them have not previously used indexing and abstracting tools, or at least are unfamiliar with the music sources of this type. With the emergence of electronic databases, the resources in this category are constantly changing, and one of the challenges of teaching a course such as this is for the teacher to stay current. Since some students will not find much information on their research topic until they begin searching for journal articles, it is important to get them to this stage as quickly as possible, within reason. This means a lot of work in daily assignments in the first part of the semester, but this often works in the students' favor, and even moderately diligent students will have a good start on the information-gathering phase of their research by mid-semester.

As students become acquainted with the various reference sources in music, it is important that they learn to evaluate them, and also that they be encouraged to organize their notes on the sources in some way so that they will be useful in the future. To this end a source worksheet can be helpful. (See Appendix D.) Students are encouraged to fill one out for each source that they study during the course. Some of the assignments specify the sources for which this is strongly recommended. Having "open book" exams and quizzes provides an added incentive for the students to make good use of the worksheets. Collecting and grading them is not recommended, since this can be extremely time consuming and not particularly valuable for the teacher or the students. To demonstrate how to use the worksheet effectively, have the students use it first in class to evaluate one source together. The *New Grove Dictionary* works well for this, as each student can peruse a different volume and hunt for examples relevant to the discussion. Most students are already somewhat familiar with this work, and can quickly assess many aspects of it in the process of filling out the worksheet as a group. It also works well to have students report on some of the assigned sources in class, and share copies of their worksheets. This is a good way to cover many sources without resorting to an undue amount of work for the students. It also gives the students a chance to explore a few sources in depth for a topic that interests them. See Appendixes E and F for two sample assignments from this unit.

Editions of Music

The main objective of this section of the course is for the students to gain a better understanding of primary sources for the study of music, and the challenges they often present for the researcher. The students should also develop their skills as critical thinkers and consumers as they choose editions of music for their own study, or with which to instruct their students. This unit can be organized in a variety of ways; one plan that works well is to begin with a discussion of primary sources, such as manuscripts and printed editions over which the composer likely had some control. Here it is essential that the students learn to make productive use of thematic catalogs. Unfortunately, foreign languages are often a barrier to students using and understanding these sources, so it is beneficial to guide them through one entry with a detailed assignment and class discussion. The example found in Appendix G is based on the Schmieder second-edition entry for Bach's *Die Kunst der Fuge*.[14] Students are often afraid of this source, especially if they do not know German, but with a glossary of common thematic catalog terms in hand, they are usually able to find some basic information. It is well worth the class time to go over the descriptions of the autograph manuscript and the first printed edition in detail, with explanations of exactly what is being presented there. Even students who are fluent in German learn something from this exercise, because the bibliographical terminology is usually unfamiliar. This assignment provides a good opportunity to introduce some basic information about music manuscript and printing practices before 1800. It also introduces the students to *RISM A/I*, *RISM A/II*, and the *British Union-Catalog of Early Music Printed Before the Year 1801*.[15, 16, 17]

The second topic of the Editions portion of the course focuses on Collected Works sets and other critical editions. The objective is for the students to gain an understanding of the collected and critical editions, their history, purposes, and limitations. If the library resources are available, have the students explore the work of a composer for whom there are two collected editions, such as J. S. Bach, Mozart, or Beethoven, so that the students can observe how the concepts and editorial practices for these editions have changed over time. James Grier's book on music editing offers a very helpful source for this topic.[18] Discussion of critical editions flows naturally into discussion of the editing practices of the more practical performance editions as well. This offers an excellent opportunity for performers to apply their evaluative and critical thinking skills to something that has practical implications for them—the selection of editions for their own use as performers and teachers. Ideally, an assignment to write a short essay comparing two different editions can be valuable at this point. Time is often short by this stage in the semester, however, and students need to spend their out-of-class time on their research papers. As an alternative, examples of variant editions of a work may be used for class discussion. The possibilities will vary with the library's collection, but a Beethoven sonata or a work from Bach's *Well-Tempered Clavier* works well for this exercise if the library has several contrasting editions available.

In this portion of the course, students also learn how to locate performance editions of music that may not be available in their local library. In early renditions of this course, students made extensive use of printed library catalogs. While these are still introduced to students, the emphasis has shifted to searching OCLC's *WorldCat* database and the online catalogs of major music libraries. The *Music in Print* series is also introduced here.

Finding information about composers who are currently active, and locating performance materials for their music, presents some special challenges. Class sessions devoted to this topic near the end of the semester provide the opportunity to review some sources that should be familiar by then, and also to delve into some sources that have not been emphasized earlier in the semester, such as databases covering current newspapers. Since the Internet often provides valuable information on contemporary composers, research in this area also provides an opportunity to discuss Internet search tools and techniques, as well as the importance of evaluating Internet sites. The assignment devised for this topic (Appendix H) calls into use many of the skills that the students have been acquiring and refining throughout the semester, and has often been used as a portion of the take-home final exam for the course.

The Third Strand: Mechanics of Research Paper Writing

The mechanics of writing may be the least engaging strand of the course, but important, nevertheless. Before teaching such a course, one would naturally want to consult with the faculty to determine their preferred style manual, and whether there are specific requirements for theses and doctoral dissertations.[19] For the teaching of bibliographic style, present concepts in small doses, introducing examples for each type of situation as it arises. Thus, the students begin with basic book citation while hunting for books in the library catalog. When dictionaries and encyclopedias are introduced, they learn how to cite an individual article from sources such as *The New Grove Dictionary*. The lessons on how to locate articles also include instruction in proper citation of a journal article and an article in a *Festschrift*. Citations for manuscripts and printed editions of music can be especially complex, and the examples for scores and sound recordings in the style manuals may not be adequate. Handouts providing supplemental examples are strongly recommended.

The mechanics of research paper writing also include making appropriate use of sources, whether with exact quotations or summary, and the proper acknowledgment of those sources through footnotes or endnotes. Some students have great difficulty with this aspect of paper writing, so Paper Preparation Assignment no. 2 is an exercise in quotation, summary, and footnoting. (See Appendix C1.) This assignment is preceded by a class discussion on avoiding plagiarism by quoting or summarizing correctly, and the proper use of footnotes to acknowledge sources.[20] Even with class discussions and examples, this is still a difficult assignment for many students, but essential in helping them achieve both a smooth research writing style and a sense of academic integrity.

Added Attractions: Optional Topics to Include in the Course

Special Collections and Archives

While most of this course will necessarily focus on the use of resources commonly found on the reference shelves and in the general collections of most music libraries, students will also benefit by examining primary sources—materials that are commonly housed in the special collections and archives of a library. Graduate students need to understand and appreciate what these materials are, how they may be used in research, and why they should be preserved. A visit to Special Collections to have a close look at manuscripts and early printed editions, or letters from earlier centuries, rarely fails to engage the interest of students.[21] This might be combined with a class session on the history of music printing. Even if your library has little music in its special collections, you may be able to locate some primary source materials that would be of interest to the students, such as letters and documents of a historical figure, or the manuscript materials of a writer.

A visit to such a facility often gives rise to many questions about the preservation of books and music. This is an excellent topic for a guest lecture if the appropriate expertise is available.

Copyright Issues in Music

All musicians should have some understanding of copyright laws as they relate to music performance and publication, and a class session devoted to this topic can be of great value. This topic grows increasingly complex, and students often have many challenging questions. One excellent source is the Music Library Association's website on copyright.[22] Consider inviting a guest lecturer if an expert is available locally.

Some Practical Considerations

Course Grading

The course paper should be the central assignment for the semester and the most important source for the course grade. Crowding the semester with many additional assignments and exams detracts from the research process, while adding tremendously to the teacher's time commitment for grading. Eliminating exams or quizzes altogether and making the course paper and related assignments a very large portion of the course grade allows the students to spend a lot more of their time on their papers, with excellent results for those who take the research paper seriously. Eliminating other exams and assignments completely, however, makes it difficult to assess the students' mastery of skills not related directly to the paper, and penalizes students who find writing difficult. A balance between the two extremes is recommended. Appendix A includes a sample grading distribution that has been used successfully.

Teaching Personnel

The ideal teacher for this course is a music librarian with substantial experience in music research. A broad knowledge of music reference sources, both paper and electronic, is essential. A solid knowledge of general electronic resources is also helpful. Though there are comparatively few music-specific databases available, much can be gleaned from electronic sources with broad coverage in the arts and humanities. If a music librarian is not available to teach the course, or to teach all sections of it, one alternative that is often considered is to have the course taught by a member of the academic teaching faculty. In this case, a librarian should be available to work with the class, perhaps as a guest presenter for class sessions on some of the resources. Keep in mind that much of the real learning of the course takes place as students use the library resources and do the necessary research for their papers, and they will have many questions as they work through this process. Reference staff are thus necessarily involved as informal on-site teachers, and should be aware of the goals and assignments of the course.

When considering possible teaching staff for this type of course, some workload issues need to be kept in mind. Teaching this course requires a tremendous amount of time, especially when course materials are first being developed. Reusing materials in later semesters can save some time, but handouts need to be updated to reflect new resources and recent editions, and a repeat can be tedious for the teacher unless there is a chance to try out some new ideas and keep the course fresh. A significant time investment is devoted to working with students and providing timely feedback as they work through the various stages of the research process. The teacher must be able to commit the necessary time to allow for a quick turnaround on paper grading, so that students are not hampered in moving to the next step of the process. If a librarian is teaching the course, there needs to be a common understanding with the library administration as to how this teaching responsibility relates to the rest of the librarian's duties. Is this an added duty, with extra pay? If so, is there an expectation that the necessary work will be done outside of normal work hours? Is the pay really sufficient to account for all of the time that the course will take? Even if the course is an added duty with extra pay, the teacher may need some flexibility in scheduling to balance teaching responsibilities with other library duties. If no extra pay is involved, the time required to teach this course needs to be considered a major portion of the librarian's job during the semesters that it is taught, and this needs to be factored in when considering the overall staffing of the library. Teaching a graduate course and running a library are two very different types of jobs. Attempting to do too much of both at once can lead to librarian burnout, with the eventual result that neither job is done well.

Team teaching is also a possibility that offers some advantages, if handled carefully.[23] A good model for handling a large enrollment involves two librarians sharing the course, dividing the class into two sub-sections for grading purposes, so that each student works with the same teacher throughout the semester. Team teaching can be an effective way to spread out the workload, and can bring more expertise and varying viewpoints to the course. Splitting a large class into smaller groups is also advantageous for hands-on work with library resources. When not formally team teaching, enlist the aid of willing colleagues for this purpose.

Class Size

Typical class sizes can range from six to thirty-five students. The optimal seems to be a class size of around nine to twelve students. In this size range, there are enough students to have good, lively class discussions without overtaxing the library's resources for their assignments, and it also provides a reasonable workload of paper grading for the teacher. This is a luxury that a large graduate program cannot afford, however. A much larger class size can also work well, provided that the teacher is given enough time and flexibility during the workday to keep up with mountains of paper grading and to work with students who have questions. Another factor to consider is the makeup of the student body you are serving. If many of your students are not native speakers of English, or are students with poor writing skills, the time required for grading papers will be much greater, and you will also likely need to spend more time working with students outside of class.

Library resources should also be considered when setting limits on class size. This course will tend to make heavy demands on the reference collection and on certain types of materials in the general collection, especially if a lot of students are doing the assignments at the same time. If large classes are necessary, consider purchasing multiple copies of key reference sources, and be sure to keep the course in mind when considering how many simultaneous users to allow for in the licensing of electronic databases.

Class Scheduling

The ideal schedule consists of two ninety-minute class periods per week. This allows enough class time to cover topics well and encourage class discussion. If the classroom is located in or near the library, or if library resources can be brought to the classroom, part of the class time can also be used for students to work individually or in small groups with the resources while the teacher is available to answer questions. With more than two class sessions per week, students have difficulty finding sufficient time between classes to use the resources on their own and to keep up with the daily assignments. This is a particular challenge when teaching this as a five- or six-week summer course with long class periods every day. To teach this course in such a compact time frame, one must mix lectures, class discussion, and individual or group work into most class sessions. A small class size is essential for this intensive approach, ideally with exceptionally motivated students.

The Research Course in the Graduate Curriculum

At the end of this course, students are asked to provide some type of written evaluation; class discussion also elicits candid comments. One of the comments heard most often is that the students found the course quite valuable, but wish they had taken it earlier in their graduate studies, or even as undergraduates. This course can easily gain a reputation among students as time-consuming and difficult, with the result that students tend to put it off until near the end of their programs. Convey to graduate advisors the wisdom of encouraging students to take this course early in their graduate programs, so that they can gain maximum benefit from it for their other coursework. This also means that the course needs to be offered often enough that students can schedule it in their first or second semester of graduate study.

CONCLUSION

Teaching this type of course can be difficult and time consuming, but it can also be tremendously rewarding for teacher and students alike, when planned carefully and approached enthusiastically. By integrating the study of the process of research, the specific tools of music research, and the mechanics of a good research paper, the teacher can create a course that engages the students in the centuries-old conversation that is music research. While the research project undertaken within a one-semester course is necessarily limited in scope, a well-designed course should help reasonably diligent students to acquire the necessary skills, understanding, and confidence to pursue more extensive research projects as their music careers develop, and to communicate their results through writing, teaching, or performing.

The opportunity to teach such a course can also be of great benefit to the teacher-librarian. While many librarians have the opportunity to teach students in a "one-shot" approach through some type of course-related bibliographic instruction, teaching a full course, especially at the graduate level, is a very different experience. When working with a group of students for the semester, the teacher receives constant feedback on the success or failure of a given lesson, assignment, or teaching technique, and can make modifications as needed in order to achieve the learning objectives. The opportunity to see a student project grow from a vague, unformed idea to a coherent and even thought-provoking research paper is the best reward for the hard work and dedication required for the successful teaching of this type of course.

APPENDIXES

Following are some sample handouts, assignments, and other materials that may be useful to the teacher planning this course for the first time. This is not a complete representation of all materials for the course.

Appendix A: General Information

This is given to students on the first day of class to serve as an overview of policies and procedures for the course.

[Course Title]—General Information
[Times. Location.]

Instructor
[Name, Title; Office Phone; Office location; E-mail; Office hours.] If you have a special need because of a physical or learning disability, please meet with your instructor early in the semester to discuss your needs.

Grading: Your grade in the course will come from the following components:

Course Paper:	40%
Three paper preparation assignments:	15% total
Quiz & score bibliography:	10%
Final exam:	15%
Class participation and other assignments:	20%
Total:	100%

Daily assignments: In addition to the paper and the "Preparation Assignments" leading up to it, there will be exercises to prepare and discuss in class. A few will be turned in for grades. You are encouraged to work together on daily class preparation, but written assignments to be turned in should be your own work. **Most of the real learning in this course takes place in the Reference area of the library, as you acquaint yourself with sources through the daily assignments and the research paper.** I would like to keep the written assignments to a minimum, and focus more on class participation and discussion as a means of active learning and feedback. The success of this, however, will depend on your willingness to participate **actively**.

Due dates: All work is due at class time on the day assigned unless an extension is arranged in consultation with the instructor before that date. **Papers and major assignments turned in late without prior permission will automatically receive a lowered grade.** Papers and assignments are always welcomed early, of course.

Daily handouts: If you miss a class, it is your responsibility to obtain missed handouts from the instructor. This course involves a lot of handouts to guide you through the various sources. Keeping your collection of course materials complete and organized will save you a lot of time.

Required texts: You are required to purchase the following, **and bring them to every class.** Copies are available at the University bookstore.

Turabian, Kate L. *A Manual for Writers of Term Papers, Theses, and Dissertations*, 6th ed., rev. by John Grossman and Alice Bennett. Chicago Guides to Writing, Editing, and Publishing. Chicago: University of Chicago Press, 1996.
This is based on the *Chicago Manual of Style*, used by many scholarly publishers in the field of music.

Booth, Wayne C., Gregory G. Colomb, and Joseph M. Williams. *The Craft of Research*, 2nd ed. Chicago Guides to Writing, Editing, and Publishing. Chicago: University of Chicago Press, 2003.
Reading assignments during the semester will guide you through the entire book at least once, and it will be featured frequently in class discussions.

Suggested text:
Duckles, Vincent, and Ida Reed. *Music Reference and Research Materials: An Annotated Bibliography*, 5th ed. New York: Schirmer Books, 1997. Ref. ML113.D83 1997.
This is also available for purchase, or you may use the copy in the library. "Duckles" has long been considered the definitive source of its kind in the field of music. The edition by Ida Reed upholds this tradition, while at the same time reflecting the tremendous changes that are taking place in the research library world. If you can afford it, this would be an excellent addition to your personal library.

Other sources: The following manuals, available in the reference area, may provide further assistance with questions of bibliographic and writing style.

The Chicago Manual of Style, 15th ed. Chicago: University of Chicago Press, 2003. Ref. Z253.U69.
Manual upon which Turabian is based, and useful for further examples or explanations.
Holoman, D. Kern. *Writing about Music: A Style Sheet from the Editors of "19th Century Music."* Berkeley: University of California Press, 1988. Ref. ML63.W68 1988.
Wingell, Richard J. *Writing about Music: An Introductory Guide*, 3rd ed. Upper Saddle River: Prentice Hall, 2002. Ref. ML3797 .W54 2002.
This is highly recommended, especially if you have not written a research paper before, or feel less than completely confident of your ability to write in the English language.

Source notebook: During the course, you will be using and evaluating a great many reference tools in the music library. As you do this, you will be recording your observations about these sources on worksheets. Some of these might be turned in as daily assignments. These will also be useful for the quizzes, since they will be "open book" exercises. For some assignments, each class member will be asked to prepare a worksheet on a different source, for distribution to all class members. This will spread the workload, and allow you to study some sources in more depth.

A word on writing: Your papers and written assignments will be graded on style as well as content. Spelling, grammar, and typing accuracy do count when you are trying to convey your ideas to others via the written word. **Always allow time to proofread and edit your work.** Writing research papers in English can be difficult, especially (but not exclusively) for those whose first language is not English. We do not expect all of you to be at the same level, but we do hope that those with weaker writing skills will make an effort at improvement during this course. Such improvement will be taken into account in the grading of your final paper.

Appendix B: Basic Schedule

While this has been presented to the students as a class-by-class schedule specific to the calendar of the semester, the following is a more generic week-by-week schedule showing the main learning objectives, activities, and assignments for each week.

Week One

Learning Objectives	To gain an overview of the course and the course paper. To understand the different types and purposes of research. To begin exploring the various types of research found in the field of music, both historic and current. To understand the functions of a library catalog, and to gain a basic understanding of the principles that make it work for the searcher. To become an efficient searcher in the home library's catalog and begin exploring materials available for a possible paper topic.

Reading Assignments	*Craft of Research,* Part I; articles on musicology in *New Grove* and *New Harvard Dictionary of Music.*
Other Assignments	Exercise on searching the library catalog for materials by and about a composer of the student's choice, being considered as a possible paper topic.
Class Activities	Course overview; presentation and discussion of catalog principles (uniform titles for music, use of name headings, subject headings and classification, keyword vs. browse searching); hands-on catalog search training in library instruction lab.

Week Two

Learning Objectives	Continue objectives of Week One. To understand why citation style is important; to be able to cite properly a book and a signed article in a subject encyclopedia. To gain a general understanding of the growth of research literature in a given field. To begin exploring the research literature about music, starting with dictionaries and encyclopedias.
Reading Assignments	*Craft of Research,* Part II, prologue and chapters 3–4. *New Grove* article "Dictionaries and Encyclopedias of Music."
Other Assignments	Begin work on paper topic proposals; explore selected dictionaries and encyclopedias of music, preparing source worksheets for assigned titles, including one or two to share with class.
Class Activities	Review catalog exercise in class. Discuss readings from Week One. Discuss reading assignment for Week Two, especially as it

relates to the preparation of the paper topic proposal. Introduce concept of source worksheets; bring volumes of *New Grove* to class and fill out the worksheet for it as a group. Class presentation/discussion on how to evaluate a printed source. Short presentation with examples of citation style.

Week Three

Learning Objectives	To develop skills in assessing and evaluating reference sources, using dictionaries and encyclopedias in music as examples. To understand the concepts of primary, secondary, and tertiary sources, and their respective roles and uses in the research process. To begin developing a strategy for finding research materials related to the paper topic. To explore composer bibliographies and to gain a basic understanding of the importance of thematic catalogs to music research. To learn ways to access books and dissertations not available through the library's catalog.
Reading Assignments	*Craft of Research,* Part II, chapters 5–6.
Other Assignments	Paper topic proposal due. Class reports on selected dictionaries and encyclopedias. Begin working with bibliographies devoted to single composers. Begin exploring on-line databases: *Books in Print, WorldCat,* and *Dissertation Abstracts*.
Class Activities	Class reports. Presentation/discussion on composer bibliographies and thematic catalogs and their history. Introduction to databases.

Week Four

Learning Objectives	To understand the importance of journal articles as a record of the ongoing research conversation. To be able to use paper and electronic indexing and abstracting tools to locate journal articles on a music topic. To be able to cite journal articles properly. To understand the concept of "collected essay" publications such as *Festschriften*, and how to locate and cite articles in such collections. To begin exploring the parts of a research argument as set forth in *Craft of Research*: claims, reasons, evidence, acknowledgments and responses, warrants, qualifications.
Reading Assignments	*Craft of Research*, Part III, prologue and chapters 7–11. Read assigned article for class discussion in Week Five, as an example of "research argument" concepts.
Other Assignments	Use the various indexing tools to locate articles on paper topic; prepare source worksheets on selected tools.
Class Activities	Presentation/discussion on importance of journal articles to research; history and importance of indexing and abstracting tools. Hands-on training on use of online tools. Principles of citation for journal articles, including handout with examples from music journals. Introduction to "research argument" concepts.

Week Five

Learning Objectives	Continue objectives from Week Four; explore sources on performance practice and notation.

Reading Assignments	No new assignments.
Other Assignments	Source worksheets on performance practice and notation sources. Gather citations for Paper Preparation Assignment no. 1.
Class Activities	Class discussion of the assigned article and *Craft of Research*, Part III. Short discussion of literature on performance practice and notation. Class discussion and questions about literature bibliographies. This is a good time to review evaluation of sources and make sure that students understand what types of sources are or are not appropriate for their research papers.

Week Six

Learning Objectives	To further develop understanding of bibliographic citation. To learn the basic history of musical sound recordings and their place in music research, and to explore the basic discographical sources. To learn basic principles of citation for sound recordings. To explore bibliographies devoted to particular instruments, genres, or subjects in music.
Reading Assignments	None.
Other Assignments	Literature bibliography practice citations to be turned in; prepare literature bibliography for graded assignment due next week. Source worksheets for discography sources.
Class Activities	Presentation/discussion on sound recordings and discography sources. Individual/small group work with subject/genre bibliographies for reporting in class next week.

Week Seven

Learning Objectives — To learn the elements of good paper writing, including proper use of quotation, summary, footnoting, etc. To understand the ethical issues of research what constitutes plagiarism, and how to avoid it. To solidify knowledge of literature about music.

Reading Assignments — *Craft of Research*, pp. 201–7 and 285–88.

Other Assignments — Paper Preparation Assignment no. 1 (literature bibliography) due.

Class Activities — Presentation/discussion on paper writing, quotation, footnoting, plagiarism, etc. Review for quiz on literature sources.

Week Eight

Learning Objectives — To understand the types and uses of primary sources relating to editions of musical works. To understand the history and importance of thematic catalogs. To gain an initial acquaintance with *RISM* and its significance to music research. To learn the basic principles of citation for printed and manuscript music.

Reading Assignments — Background readings in *New Grove* on thematic catalogs, and *RISM*.

Other Assignments — Assignment using Schmieder thematic catalog, *RISM*, and *The British Union-Catalogue of Early Music Printed Before the Year 1801* to locate primary sources for a work. (See Appendix G for example.)

Class Activities — Quiz on literature sources. Presentation/discussion on primary sources in music; use of thematic catalogs, *RISM*, etc. Class discussion on questions about upcoming

Paper Preparation Assignment (quotation, footnoting, etc.).

Week Nine

Learning Objectives	To demonstrate effective use of quotation, summary, and footnoting. To demonstrate effective use of a thematic catalog in German, *RISM* A/I and A/II, and the *British Union-Catalogue* to locate information about manuscripts and early printed editions of music. To understand the history and importance of collected editions in music. To gain an understanding and appreciation for the tools that aid the researcher in locating specific works in collected editions and monumental series.
Reading Assignments	*New Grove* article, "editing." Grier, preface and chapter 1.[24]
Other Assignments	Paper Preparation Assignment no. 2 (Quotation/summary, footnoting); assignment on collected editions, use of Heyer, and basic comparison of two editions.[25]
Class Activities	Detailed discussion in class on Schmieder/*RISM* assignment. Introductory discussion on collected editions; evaluation and comparison of editions of music.

Week Ten

Learning Objectives	To demonstrate an understanding of collected editions and their place in music research. To understand the different purposes of music editions (both "scholarly"

	and "practical") and to learn how to evaluate them for different purposes and needs. To understand proper citation style for works in collected editions and series.
Reading Assignments	None.
Other Assignments	Begin work on score citations for practice assignment due next week.
Class Activities	Discuss assignment on collected editions, use of Heyer, and comparison of editions. Class discussion on citation style for scores, with examples to complete in class. Session on searching library catalogs and *WorldCat* in library computer classroom.

Week Eleven

Learning Objectives	To gain a basic understanding of the history of music printing, and its influence on the course of music history and society. To become acquainted with the particular challenges of researching music of pre-baroque periods, and the basic resources that help to meet those challenges. To gain an understanding and appreciation of library special collections and archives, and their importance to music researchers.
Reading Assignments	None.
Other Assignments	Score practice citations due. Continue individual work on research papers.
Class Activities	Class presentation on history of printing and sources for the study of early (pre-baroque) music. Visit to Library Special Collections.

Week Twelve

Learning Objectives	To demonstrate progress on research for paper; to begin learning how to outline and draft a paper. To begin exploring the special challenges and sources for research in contemporary music.
Reading Assignments	*Craft of Research*, Part IV.
Other Assignments	Score bibliography assignment due.
Class Activities	Class discussion and informal progress reports on research papers. Presentation and discussion on outlining, drafting, etc. Presentation and beginning discussion on sources and strategies for research on contemporary music.

Week Thirteen

Learning Objectives	To demonstrate significant progress on the course research paper, and the ability to organize ideas for an effective research argument. To become familiar with online tools and resources that are especially useful for research in contemporary music. To be able to search the Internet effectively, and to evaluate Internet resources. To be able to cite correctly materials from online databases and the Internet.
Reading Assignments	None.
Other Assignments	Paper Preparation Assignment no. 3 (Introduction and outline or partial draft) due.
Class Activities	Class sessions in library computer classroom to work with databases and Internet search tools. Some class discussion on writing of papers may also be needed.

Week Fourteen

Learning Objectives	To gain a basic understanding of copyright issues for music and musicians. To explore other resources in music (such as sources for career information, grants, etc.).
Reading Assignments	Basic copyright law.
Other Assignments	Explore the Music Library Association's copyright website.[26]
Class Activities	Presentation and discussion on copyright issues; other resources in music. [In the semester on which this outline was based, week fourteen included a holiday and only one class period.]

Week Fifteen

Learning Objectives	To complete a major research paper. To relate music research questions to musical performances.
Reading Assignments	None.
Other Assignments	Course paper due. Take-home final exam distributed.
Class Activities	Informal class presentations on research papers, including optional performances.

Appendix C: Course Paper Description

The following course paper description is given to students on the first day of class. More detailed instructions are generally needed before the preparation assignments are due, especially for Paper Preparation Assignments 2 and 3. Sample instructions for those assignments are found in Appendix C1 and Appendix C2. These are generally handed out to students a few weeks before the due date for that assignment.

[Course Title]
Course Paper: Due Week Fifteen

Choose a work by a major composer of the "Common Practice" period—the eighteenth, nineteenth, or early twentieth century. Your course work may be easier if you choose a composer for whom at least one "Collected Edition" exists in the library, and a work for which we own several performing editions in the library, but these are not requirements. Be sure to select a work that will sustain your interest over the course of the semester. You will be turning in your paper topic choice and a very preliminary list of sources in Week Three. During the semester you will be gathering various kinds of information about this work as you learn to use the many research tools available in the library. Write a paper (ca. eight to twelve pages—**no more than fifteen pages**) presenting a historical introduction to the work, and then focusing on one of the following topics:

1. Write an in-depth comparison of two or more different editions of the work, providing as much information as you can about the origins of each edition—who the editors were, the apparent purpose of each edition, etc. You will want to include a study of any manuscript or early printed sources that are available in facsimile in the library. Criteria for comparing editions will be the focus of class discussion and an assignment during the semester. Performance issues and historical practices will most likely also be a part of your research and discussion.
2. Discuss performance practice issues as evidenced in a few important recordings of the work. You will want to include relevant background material on the performers and the history of each recording. For this option to work well, you will need to think carefully about what criteria you will use to compare the recordings. You will probably want to consult reviews of the recordings you are comparing, but be aware that recording reviews may not be good models for research paper writing style.

3. If neither of the above options appeals to you, or works well for the piece you have chosen, consider taking a more historical approach, such as: a) an in-depth "publication history" of the work, from its earliest known manuscript sources to the present day; b) a history of the reception of the work—through reviews, personal accounts, etc.; c) an in-depth look at the historical context of the work. What else was going on when it was written, in the composer's life? In music? In other arts? In politics? How do these factors relate to the work, directly or indirectly?

Warning: For some of the choices in option 3, you may need to go beyond the confines of our music library for research. For any topic in option 3, you should consult with your instructor as you plan your research.

What this paper should definitely **not** be is a theoretical analysis. You may need to include a theoretical concept to demonstrate and support a claim, but save the complete analysis for a theory course.

No recycling! It is against the policy of this course to turn in the same, or a similar paper that you have also turned in or are turning in for another course. You may research the same topic for two different papers, but the resulting papers must be on different aspects of the topic.

No matter what topic approach you choose, your paper should, of course, be well documented and properly footnoted (or endnoted). Class discussion and preparatory exercises will be included on this during the semester. In addition to the eight- to twelve-page text, all papers are to include a complete and well-formatted bibliography of the sources you consulted, including books, journal articles, scores, and sound recordings as applicable.

The following assignments are designed to lead you through the process of writing a research paper and the mechanics of preparing a good bibliography. Details will be discussed in class well before each assignment is due. These descriptions will give you some idea of what is expected.

Paper Preparation Assignment no. 1: Due Week Seven

Prepare a "working" or preliminary bibliography of literature on your paper topic, i.e. books, articles, etc. Citations should be in alphabetical order by author or editor, and should follow the Turabian bibliographical style manual precisely. In compiling this bibliography, you will need to be selective. The object is **not** to list everything ever written, but to choose the sources that you think will be useful for your research. (At this point you probably will not yet know what will **really** be useful to you. This is a preliminary bibliography that may change considerably by the final paper.) Record jackets and CD liner notes are **not** acceptable sources for a research paper. Reviews of recordings should be used sparingly.

Paper Preparation Assignment no. 2: Due Week Nine

For this assignment you will write one or two paragraphs of background information on your paper topic, in which you demonstrate at least one example of exact quotation of another author's words, and one example of summarizing another author's ideas **entirely in your own words.** You will also demonstrate proper footnoting practice and style.

Paper Preparation Assignment no. 3: Due Week Thirteen

At this point you will prepare a detailed outline of your paper, along with a "working introduction" or partial draft.

More details on these assignments will be provided later.

Appendix C1: Quotation, Summary, and Footnoting Assignment

As mentioned above, this assignment can be very difficult for students who are inexperienced in research writing. A short example based on a familiar source (such as an article read and discussed as a class) can be helpful as a model.

[Course Title]
Graded assignment due Week Nine.
Paper Preparation Assignment no. 2 (Quotation, Summary and Footnoting).

To prepare for this assignment, first read *Craft of Research*, pp. 201-7 and 285-88. **Read the "Quick Tip," pp. 205-7 several times!** Also read through Turabian, chapter 5 for more tips on the mechanics of quoting and footnoting.

Write one or two paragraphs of background information on your paper topic (such as might be useful in an introduction, for example) in which you demonstrate at least one example of exact quotation of another author's words, and one example of summarizing another author's ideas **entirely in your own words.** Be sure to properly footnote (or endnote) your source in each case, following the principles outlined in chapter 8 of Turabian, and using the "N" examples in chapter 11 as models. Typing/word processing is strongly preferred for this assignment. **Please photocopy the sources you quote and summarize, and include them when you turn in the assignment. (It will not be graded without this material.)**

Appendix C2: Introduction and Outline Assignment

[Course Title]
Assignment due by Week Thirteen.
Introduction and Outline (Paper Preparation Assignment no. 3).

By now you should have gathered a fair amount of research material on your topic, and should be well along in the process of studying that material for its possible application to your own research project. At this point, you need to begin planning and drafting your paper. This is a process in which everyone works in different ways, and at a different pace. Some of you may be able at this point to produce a complete, well-written introduction and detailed outline of your complete argument and supporting evidence, while others may still be working on better defining your topics. This assignment should help you (and me) to see where you are in the process, what you intend to "prove" in your paper, and to formulate at least a general plan that will convey your findings effectively to your reader. If you find yourself floundering at this point on what direction to take with your paper, or what to do next, I **strongly** encourage you to make an appointment to meet with me.

Background Reading

In *Craft of Research*, read Part IV, and reread the section in Part V on The Ethics of Research, i.e., through page 288.

Outline

Prepare an outline for the paper you are planning. A point-based outline, as presented on pp. 187–88 of *Craft of Research* would be a good model.

Introduction

As the authors of *Craft of Research* point out, you may not be able to write a complete, polished introduction to your paper until you have a revised draft of the rest of it. However, you should be able to provide a "working introduction" that begins with some context for your paper, then states your research problem and some sense of a possible solution. (See pp. 195–96 in *C of R*.)

Alternative

If you prefer, you may turn in a partial (or complete) draft of your paper for this assignment. It **must** be enough to show where you are going with the paper: what your major claims and evidence will be, how you are organizing your argument, etc. You would probably find it helpful to outline anyway, to get an objective sense of your paper's organization.

Appendix D: Source Worksheet

As explained in the text, the source worksheet is a device to assist the students in recording their observations about sources they study during the semester, and to help them keep their information organized.[27] This is introduced with a class exercise using *New Grove* as an example. Here is an example of how the source worksheet might be filled out for *New Grove*, second edition.

Source Worksheet
Source type: Encyclopedia
Call no.: Ref. ML100. N
Brief title: *New Grove Dictionary*
Bibliographic citation (Turabian style):
Sadie, Stanley, ed. *The New Grove Dictionary of Music and Musicians*, 2nd ed. 29 vols. New York: Grove, 2001.

Purpose and scope: Has articles on broad range of topics in music, including composers, performers, publishers, countries, major cities, musical instruments, musical terminology and concepts. Articles for major composers are extensive. According to comments in the preface to the revised edition: expanded from previous edition by about 50 percent. Not cumulative—some articles in 1980 edition are now of less interest and have been dropped. Expanded coverage of twentieth-century composers; more inclusion of popular music; many added topics.

Important strengths: In-depth articles on many topics in music. Extensive bibliographies. Articles for major composers include comprehensive and detailed lists of works, often organized by genre and including catalog numbers and references to complete works sets. Lots of black and white illustrations, including manuscript reproductions.

Weaknesses or limitations: Illustrations not in color. Printed edition cannot remain "current."

Other comments on content: Available online; online version can be updated. Related works such as *New Grove Dictionary of American Music*, *New Grove Dictionary of Jazz*, *New Grove Dictionary of Musical Instruments*, and *New Grove Dictionary of Opera* provide expanded coverage in those areas.

Type of arrangement: Alphabetical.

Indexes: "Thematic" index in vol. 29. Not intended to be a full-text index; aims to show topical relationships between articles. Includes lists of composers, performers, and writers by time period.

Special features: Each volume includes lists of abbreviations and library sigla (important for in-depth research). Appendixes in vol. 28: Collections (Private) — includes brief descriptions; Congress Reports — bibliography by year; Dictionaries and Encyclopedias of Music — chronological list and index; Editions (Historical) — bibliographies of single-composer editions, other collected editions, and anthologies; Libraries — listed by geographical area; Periodicals — list by geographical area, with index; Sound Archives — by geographical area.

Appendix E: Dictionaries and Encyclopedias in Music

This is a lengthy assignment. The "Sources for Study" section below generally lists around thirty to thirty-five examples of dictionaries and encyclopedias on music, organized by category. In this appendix, the actual citations have not been included.

[Course Title: Weeks Two and Three]
Terminology and Background Material: Dictionaries & Encyclopedias in Music.

Background Reading:
New Grove Dictionary of Music, 2nd ed. Vol. 7. "Dictionaries and Encyclopedias of Music."

Sources for study: The student assignment generally lists around eighteen to twenty sources in the first five sections, of which nine to ten are marked for more detailed study. Each item listing includes the library call number and the item number from Duckles and Reed.[28] A similar format is used for source-related assignments throughout the semester. The categories used are:

- Terminology: General Music Dictionaries and Glossaries.
- Multi-Volume Encyclopedias.
- Single-Volume Encyclopedias.
- Biographical Dictionaries.
- Miscellaneous.
- Special Subject Dictionaries and Encyclopedias. [The topics included in this section vary by semester, according to the performance areas of the students. Examples include sources on jazz, opera, piano, popular music, singers, women musicians. Most of the class report assignments are made from this section. Groups of two or three students are often assigned to work together on a category. Some class time is provided for them to begin their work as a group.]

Assignment: (mainly for class discussion)

1. Examine the sources listed above. Prepare worksheets for those marked * on the handout. Looking up the same term or topic in two or more similar sources is a good way to make some concrete observations about content, depth of coverage, and so forth.

2. In addition to the sources marked *, you may be assigned one of the nonmarked sources to explore in depth and report on **briefly** to the class on Tuesday. As part of your report, you are to prepare a source worksheet to be copied and distributed to the class.
3. Also browse Reference ML100—ML105 and find a source **not listed above** that interests you. Prepare a source worksheet for your own use. **Bring the source to class on Tuesday and be prepared to talk about it very briefly.** (You do not need to provide copies of the worksheet for everyone.)
4. Look up your course paper composer in all applicable sources listed above, and any others you find on the Reference shelves as time permits. Also look up any terminology that might be related to your topic. Compare the treatment of the various sources and begin to compile useful background information and bibliographical "leads" for your paper.

Appendix F: Composer-Based Bibliographies and Other Access to Books and Dissertations

[Course Title: Week Three]
Composer-Based Bibliographies and Other Access to Books and Dissertations in Music

Composer-Based Bibliographies

Explore the ML134 area in Reference, and also in the general collection. It is suborganized alphabetically by composer. Here you may find thematic catalogs and other bibliographies devoted to the composer you are studying. (Not all composers have a thematic catalog or bibliography yet, however.) Also see Duckles & Reed, chapter 6, especially the list by composer beginning on page 338. Study any sources you find about your composer and prepare source worksheets for those that look particularly useful. **Be prepared to briefly describe the most useful source(s) in class.** While studying them, you will, of course want to be looking for leads to useful materials for your paper. If your composer is not represented in ML134, pick one that is and survey what is there.

A note about **thematic catalogs:** We will be studying these in greater depth later in the semester. For now, try to locate the entry for the piece you are researching. Somewhere in the entry (often at the end) there may be a brief bibliography of literature about that work.

Access to Books and Dissertations through Online Databases

There are a growing number of online databases that provide various kinds of access to books and dissertations. Following are a few important ones that are available here. Begin to explore these on your own; we will look at these on Wednesday, when we will meet in the library computer classroom.

- **Books In Print:** General U.S. trade source primarily for finding out what is available for purchase; includes prices. Lists some out-of-print items, as well as books that have been announced but not yet published.
- **WorldCat:** This is actually a "Union" catalog of entries contributed by libraries all over the United States (and the world, to a lesser extent). We will use this more extensively when we start looking for scores. In this database you can find out which libraries own an item, and even request Interlibrary Loan directly from your search.
- **Dissertation Abstracts:** Complete range of North American academic dissertations since 1861. Lengthy abstracts.
- **RILM Abstracts:** Covers scholarly works on all aspects of music, in many formats: periodical articles, books, dissertations, conference proceedings, etc. Most entries include brief abstracts. Also have a look at the print version, in Reference. See Duckles #4.90 and 12.13.

Other Sources

See *Doctoral Dissertations in Musicology-Online* at: http://www.music.indiana.edu/ddm. DDM-Online now includes all records from Adkins & Dickinson, *Doctoral Dissertations in Musicology*, 2nd international ed. (1984), and 2nd series, 2nd cumulative ed. (1996), as well as "current records" since 1996. See the venerable paper source also, Ref. ML128.M8A4.

Appendix G: Finding First and Early Editions of Music

This assignment is accompanied by a handout recommending background readings in Brook & Viano's *Thematic Catalogues in Music*, and providing brief descriptions of the sources used in the assignment.[29] The students are also given a glossary of German terms commonly found in thematic catalogs. This is not an easy assignment, even for students who are fluent in German, and is especially difficult for those who are not. Class discussion is therefore an especially important component of learning in this case.

[Course Title]
Finding First and Early Editions of Music: Works Lists in New Grove; Thematic Catalogs; RISM; British Union Catalog ("BUC")

For this assignment, you will be looking up Johann Sebastian Bach's *Art of the Fugue (Die Kunst der Fuge)* in most of the sources listed on the assignment. Because everyone will be using the same reference books for this assignment, **please return the books to the reference table when you are finished.** You will probably find it easiest to do the assignment if you can assemble most of the sources at one time and look at them together. You may also want to work together in small groups for this assignment. **Please do not mark up these sources as you use them!**

1. Find the *New Grove* article on J. S. Bach and look in the Works list for the entry on his *Art of the Fugue*. Does an autograph manuscript exist for this work? What does the entry tell you about it? While you are here, note the BWV number of the work.
2. Find the Schmieder thematic catalog for Bach, 2nd edition. First spend a little time reading through the introductory material at the beginning of the book (in both German & English), especially the preface to the 2nd edition (p. xxxv), and Remarks (p. xlv). Also locate the list of abbreviations, pp. xxxvii–xliv, which is only in German.

    Now look up the entry for Bach's *Die Kunst der Fuge*. Near the beginning of the entry, what does it say about when and where the work was composed? (Hint: What is EZ an abbreviation for?)
3. Still in Schmieder, skim through the entire entry and try to identify the major sections with the help of the glossary provided with this assignment. Then go back to the page with information about manuscript and early printed sources. A copy of that page is attached to this assignment. This page is full of information about primary sources for this work; the language and extensive use of abbreviations can make it tough to decipher. The questions below should guide you in gleaning some of the basics.

    Find the reference to the autograph manuscript, and mark it on the photocopy. What types of information does it give you about this manuscript that *New Grove* did not?

    Find the reference to a manuscript copy made in 1755 by someone named Penzel. Mark the lines on the photocopy. What library owns this manuscript copy?
4. Now get into the *RISM* A/II online database and do a search for this work. You should find a number of entries. Study the entries that seem to be for the whole work (rather than excerpts) and try to match them up with the manuscripts listed in Schmieder. You should, for example, be able to find the copy

by Penzel. What kinds of information do you find here that you do not find in Schmieder?

5. Now go back to your Schmieder photocopy and look at the section on the first printed edition. This presents a rather detailed (and difficult to decipher) bibliographic description of the first edition and a second printing of it. Look for the title (as it was on that first edition) and two publication dates. Mark them in the photocopy. Starting in the seventh line of that paragraph, it is telling you that there are four known copies of the first edition, and sixteen of the *Titelauflage*. It then goes on to list all of the libaries holding copies. Underline all that are in the United States. Which well-known library in the United States owns two copies?

6. Also skim through the section in Schmieder on other early editions before 1850. Now go to the *British Union Catalogue* (*BUC*) and *RISM* A/I and look for entries of this work in both of those sources.

    How many entries for this work are found in *BUC*? What libraries own the edition(s) listed?

    How many entries for this work are listed in *RISM* A/I? Can you find any correlation between entries here and those in *BUC* and Schmieder? (You should find a lot of overlap, i.e. the same editions in more than one source, but the format and fullness of information may be very different among these three sources.)

7. Look at the J. S. Bach article in Eitner. This is very hard to follow if you do not know German, but skim through p. 276 until you come to the entry for *Die Kunst der Fuge*. Is this listing a manuscript or the first printed edition(s)? How can you tell? What libraries are listed as having copies? (Hint: you will need to hunt for the "Bibliotheks-Abkürzungen" near the front of the volume.)

8. If your paper topic is a work composed before about 1800, you will want to check all of the above sources for information on your piece. For later works, be sure to study the thematic catalog for your composer, if there is one.

Appendix H: Contemporary Music

The primary focus for most of the course is research on music of the "common practice" period, since this body of literature is already familiar to most music students, and since music of this period is heavily represented in most of the standard types of research sources in music. Research on contemporary music utilizes many of the same types of sources, but also presents some special challenges. This topic also lends itself well to exploration and evaluation of Internet sites. This assignment works well as a relatively easy and enjoyable take-home final exam. A more complete listing of sources that accompanies the assignment has been omitted here.

[Course Title]
Contemporary Music

Locating information about contemporary composers: biographical, works lists, publications, recordings, etc.
Final exam, Part I: Take-home assignment on contemporary music. Due: [by final exam date.]

Please write neatly, or wordprocess. Attach an extra sheet if necessary.

Choose a composer who is currently active on a national or international level. Look up the composer in the following sources and report **briefly** on the sources' usefulness in providing information about the composer and his/her works. Of particular interest will be biographical information, works lists, publication or rental information for the music, availability of recordings, current concert activities, and reviews. (You might imagine, for example, that you are organizing a concert featuring the composer's works, and need to locate performance materials, recordings, information for program notes, etc.) The main object of this assignment is not for you to report the facts you find, but to report on **what sources were (or were not) helpful in the search, and what types of information they provide.** To some extent, this assignment will serve as a review of sources used throughout the semester.

Name of composer you are researching:

1. Print biographical sources:
   Baker's Biographical Dictionary
   Contemporary Composers (Morton & Collins)
   International Who's Who in Music
2. Check the library catalog and survey our holdings of scores, recordings, and books about the composer. You do not need to list what we have in detail, but note in general the extent of our holdings. If we do not have many scores or recordings, you might want to be on the lookout during this exercise for potential acquisitions to suggest!
3. Look for recent music periodical literature:
   RILM Abstracts
   International Index to Music Periodicals
   Music Index
4. Look for recent newspaper articles (Search one of the available newspaper databases):
5. Search for printed (or manuscript) music held by other libraries, in the following. (Do not list everything you find; do report on how much you are finding, what kinds of information, etc.)
   WorldCat
   New York Public Library (CATNYP) **OR** Library of Congress (Underline the one you have chosen.)
6. For an American composer, search the catalog of the American Music Center on the web. For a composer from another country, check the website of the International Association of Music Information Centres and look for a link to the MIC of the appropriate country.
7. Check two commercial sources on the Internet to find out what recordings of the composer's music are currently available.
8. Using the web search tool of your choice, search for websites that provide information on the composer, his works, etc. List below a few that look especially promising.

9. Now summarize your experiences with this search in a few sentences. Use the back of this sheet if needed. What would you recommend as the best search strategy for finding materials related to this composer? What did not work, and can you explain why?

NOTES

1. The author's own experience as the instructor for such a course began in the fall of 1991 at the Eastman School of Music, as one of four librarians team-teaching three sections of music bibliography. In subsequent years (through the fall of 1997), this grew into full responsibility for one section of the course, at least loosely coordinating with Mary Wallace Davidson, who was teaching the other sections. Some of the ideas presented here were likely originated by Davidson. A decade of revision and evolution has obscured their origins. The author gratefully acknowledges the contributions of Davidson, as well as Jennifer Bowen, Joan Swanekamp, and Philip Ponella, all of whom worked with the author as team teachers. Responsibility for any shortcomings in this account, however, lies solely with the present author. At the University of Houston the author taught a very similar course, entitled Introduction to Musicology, in the summer and fall semesters of 1999 and 2000. At both institutions most of the students in these courses were working on a performance degree at the Masters level, though at the University of Houston some classes have also included students in DMA programs, as well as a few pursuing a Masters in music education, musicology, or music theory.

2. Wayne C. Booth, Gregory G. Colomb, and Joseph M. Williams, *The Craft of Research*, 2nd ed. Chicago Guides to Writing, Editing, and Publishing (Chicago: University of Chicago Press, 2003), 5.

3. *The Craft of Research* is an excellent choice. It explains the process of research in a way that is understandable and entertaining, and provides an excellent foundation for this thread of the course, as well as the mechanics of research writing. The authors focus on writing as the way to communicate the results of research, but some of their ideas can easily be

applied to music performance and music editing as alternate forms of research communication that may seem more relevant to performers.

4. Booth, Colomb, and Williams in chapter 1 provide numerous examples to illustrate this, and a strong rationale for writing as a means of active learning.

5. Booth, Colomb, and Williams, 17–18.

6. Here again, the entertaining examples provided by Booth, Colomb, and Williams in chapter 2 elucidate this.

7. Vincent Duckles and Jann Pasler, "Musicology I: The Nature of Musicology," in *The New Grove Dictionary of Music and Musicians*, 2nd ed. (London: Grove, 2001).

8. Don Michael Randel, "Musicology," in *The New Harvard Dictionary of Music* (Cambridge, Mass.: The Belknap Press of Harvard University Press, 1986).

9. The discussion and examples found in Booth, Colomb, and Williams, Part III, provide a good foundation, but need to be supplemented with class discussion. Terminology used by the present author is from this source.

10. William S. Newman, "The Opening Trill in Beethoven's Sonata for Piano and Violin, Opus 96," in *Musik, Edition, Interpretation: Gedenkschrift Günter Henle*, edited by Martin Bente (Munich: G. Henle, 1980), 384–93.

11. Booth, Colomb, and Williams, chapter 11.

12. *The Creative Process*, Studies in the History of Music, vol. 3 (New York: Broude, 1992).

13. Steven Ledbetter, "Trial's Tribulations," in *The Creative Process*, Studies in the History of Music, vol. 3 (New York: Broude, 1992), 217–46.

14. Wolfgang Schmieder, *Thematisch-systematisches Verzeichnis der musikalischen Werke von Johann Sebastian Bach: Bach-Werke-Verzeichnis (BWV)*, 2. überarbeitete und erw. Ausg. (Wiesbaden: Breitkopf & Härtel, 1990), 797–803.

15. Karlheinz Schlager, *Einzeldrucke vor 1800*. 12 vols. Répertoire international des sources musicales, A I (Kassel: Bärenreiter-Verlag, 1971–).

16. *RISM: International Inventory of Musical Sources After 1600*. Répertoire international des sources musicales, A II. BiblioLine, http://biblioline.nisc.com/scripts/login.dll?BiblioLine (August 15, 2003).

17. Edith B. Schnapper, ed., *The British Union Catalogue of Early Music Printed Before the Year 1801: A Record of the Holdings of over One Hundred Libraries throughout the British Isles* (London: Butterworths Scientific Publications, 1957).

18. James Grier, *The Critical Editing of Music: History, Method, and Practice* (Cambridge: Cambridge University Press, 1996).

19. The style manual used by both institutions for which this course was developed is: Kate L. Turabian, *A Manual for Writers of Term Papers, Theses, and Dissertations*, 6th ed., rev. by John Grossman and Alice Bennett. Chicago Guides to Writing, Editing, and Publishing (Chicago: University of Chicago Press, 1996).

20. Booth, Colomb, and Williams provide useful passages on this topic, including pp. 201–7 and 285–88. The common style manuals also provide some assistance.

21. Teaching this course at the Sibley Music Library afforded access to an incomparable collection of rare music materials, as well as knowledgeable colleagues who could help to bring the collections alive to the students, but this kind of resource is exceptional. At the University of Houston, the Special Collections and Archives Department's holdings in music are not extensive, but it is a well-balanced collection that provides many fine examples illustrating music manuscript and printing practices from the fifteenth century to the present.

22. "Copyright for Music Librarians," *Music Library Association* 2003, http://www.lib.jmu.edu/org/mla/ (August 18, 2003).

23. This author's first involvement with this course was as one of a team of four librarians teaching three sections, with a total of about seventy to eighty students. This made efficient use of our time, but was confusing to the students, as their assignments were often graded by different people, and it was difficult for them to get consistent feedback as they worked through the steps of their research papers.

24. Grier, *The Critical Editing of Music*, xiii–37.

25. Anna Harriet Heyer, *Historical Sets, Collected Editions, and Monuments of Music: A Guide to Their Contents*, 3rd ed. 2 vols. (Chicago: American Library Association, 1980).

26. "Copyright for Music Librarians."

27. The worksheet shown here is modified from a model first developed with Mary Wallace Davidson.

28. Vincent H. Duckles and Ida Reed, *Music Reference and Research Materials: An Annotated Bibliography*, 5th ed. (New York: Schirmer Books, 1997).

29. Barry S. Brook and Richard Viano, *Thematic Catalogues in Music: An Annotated Bibliography*, 2nd ed. (Stuyvesant, N.Y.: Pendragon Press, 1997).

3

Reference Assistants on the Front Line in the Music Library

Kathleen A. Abromeit

Considering the many services offered in music libraries today—circulation, reserves, interlibrary loan, and reference services—librarians face a difficult balancing act. How do they provide this array of services given their densely concentrated schedules? Librarians seem to find reference service, the neediest area, given the extensive demands for individualized attention it requires.

This chapter provides an overview of a model program in an academic setting for teaching such student assistants basic reference skills so that they might attend to a variety of reference situations encountered at the music library reference desk.[1] As proven in the past two decades since the student reference assistant training program's inception at the Oberlin College Conservatory Library, students who are well trained and carefully monitored work extremely well with their peers in delivering music reference assistance.[2] What follows includes a description of the training module and its application, the method of selecting reference assistants, as well as an evaluation of the program and its role in mentoring undergraduates in the music library profession.

OVERVIEW OF REFERENCE SERVICES

Typically, a college music library reference desk is open daily to assist with in-person, telephone, or e-mail reference queries. Most often questions concern information about music (printed and recorded), books and articles, brief answers to factual questions, and suggestions for sources. All of these sorts of questions may be considered appropriate for student assistants (referred to throughout this chapter as "Reffies") to handle at the reference desk.[3] However, Reffies frequently provide service that requires a higher skill level such as identifying, locating, and using appropriate print, digital and other resources; as well as help in finding specific books, articles, music materials, and other items.[4] Of course, Reffies, who are eager to further develop their skill level in formulating and pursuing library research strategies, confer with the public services librarian regarding specific questions as they arise.

SELECTING REFERENCE ASSISTANTS

A music library reference desk that is open about thirty-five hours per week, including nights and weekends, needs a staff of eight Reffies. Music majors seem to be most appropriately prepared for this work, although it is feasible to hire students who might possess a variety of musical strengths but who may not major in music. Certainly all music library reference assistants will experience training and learn about various reference resources, but knowledge gained prior to the training is always useful as it broadens the collective knowledge base of the staff.

In preparation for fall semester, Reffies should be hired to begin their training the previous spring semester. While one might think that hiring first-year students is the most productive in terms of retention, experience suggests that hiring sophomores is actually preferable. In part, the students have had a year and a half of college experience, which seems to instill greater self-confidence in their understanding of music and the college or university environment. In addition, by the second semester of the second year they have had at least one big moment of self-doubt regarding their chosen major of study. Usually, having had this much college experience, they will have decided to leave the program or made a deeper commitment to the field. It is desirable to invest a semester of training only in those whose passion for intensive study in music has grown.

While training for Reffies takes place in the spring semester, hiring actually should take place earlier, preferably by late November. A typical posting for music library reference positions should include a short description of the job stating that the successful candidate(s) will train for service at the Reference Desk and develop knowledge of library resources and music bibliography.[5] Depending upon the specific economic situation of the institution, it may also be necessary to seek students who are eligible for financial aid or work-study positions.

With regard to the actual qualifications for these positions, however, the three most important areas of qualifications in addition to a background in music are (1) ability to work with people (to function effectively under pressure and to work cooperatively as part of a team); (2) willingness to continue learning or growing with the job and to accept increasing responsibility; and (3) reliability and punctuality.

While one can conclude a great deal about neatness, eye for detail and overall musical knowledge from an application, the interview is most important in determining the applicant's potential as a reference assistant. In interviewing for these positions, one is actually trying to determine if the student has strong interpersonal skills, as well as the capacity to develop acute critical assessment skills, the ability to work with a variety of personality types, and a broad range of musical interests. The standard list of questions is included in Appendix A.[6]

The Training

Once the new Reffies have been selected and have accepted positions, training should begin in the spring semester. All training should be conducted in a group setting, preferably in an electronic classroom within the music library itself. At the first meeting, each trainee should be given a "Training Notebook" that contains the materials needed for the module. Materials include, for example, guides for searching specific databases, a "cheat sheet" for German used in thematic catalogs, and the 048 codes used in the MARC record.[7] (See Appendix B for a list of the "Training Notebook" contents.)

Reffies should be paid for their training at a rate of two hours per week: one hour allocated for group meeting, and the other hour as time to complete the lab assignment for that week. (See details on the training schedule given in Appendix C.) Because the entire training module can be conducted in twenty-two hours, it is possible to complete the training schedule in less time than the entire semester. Accelerating the training schedule to less than a semester is not advisable, however, because trainees need that expanse of time to integrate the information and "take ownership" of it. Ultimately, the training they receive should help instill confidence and creativity in their interactions with patrons; this is difficult to achieve in a shorter period of time. Another advantage to the semester-long training is the camaraderie the students develop with one another over that period of time. This camaraderie serves them well in the future when they need to rely on each other for substitutions or other work-related "favors."

Content and Scope of the Labs

Unlike a traditional class on music bibliography that is organized around "types of sources" (such as devoting an entire unit to dictionaries or encyclopedias), the training module for music reference assistants is organized around "types of questions." As can be seen in the description of the training Labs detailed in Appendix D, for example, one week is devoted to questions in which the patron is searching for a recording of a piece of music. The training for that week should cover various ways of searching the online catalog and using discographical resources.[8]

Each lab is designed to take no more than an hour to complete, and the trainees may work alone or with a partner. While it is important that they locate answers to the questions at hand, the process used to find the answer is of primary importance. The lab should be completed at the Reffie's convenience during the week following the discussion of the specific resources. Trainees should come prepared to share both process and answers at the next scheduled training session.

Shadowing

Over the course of the training semester, there are a few weeks when no lab assignments should be made. During those weeks, the trainees should "shadow" an experienced Reffie working the reference desk. Basically, shadowing consists of sitting at the reference desk and working collaboratively with a more experienced reference assistant. This is helpful for a number of reasons. First, it provides an opportunity for the trainees and Reffies to become acquainted, as they will soon be colleagues and collaborators in this adventure. In addition, the trainees learn new ways of looking for information and observe discoveries that result from investigations made by another more experienced Reffie. It is always a good learning experience to discover that there are multiple ways to achieve the same end result.

Working the Desk

Once the reference training has been completed and the trainees have graduated, they move on to working the reference desk. During the first semester after training, the new Reffies should work at least part of their shifts when the public services librarian is available for moral support and backup. Despite the fact that they are all well trained and equipped with many safety nets, performance anxiety is common.

During a shift at the reference desk, Reffies should keep a log of all the questions they are asked and begin each shift by reading the log. The log is a helpful resource for a number of reasons. First, if a question is course-related, that question will generally be asked at least one more time. There is no reason to repeat the process used to locate the answer if a colleague has recorded the answer from an earlier shift. Another benefit to the log is that it is a vehicle for communication. The log provides a concrete illustration of any aspect of training that requires updating. The log together with electronic mail also serves as the primary communication with the public services librarian. Of course, the log is also an easy way to gather statistics.

The log also functions as a means for building a community spirit. Reffies may record appreciation for each other, a thank you for subbing, or other fun comments that help enrich their experience.[9]

As previously mentioned, new Reffies should be scheduled to work during times when the public services librarian is available for backup. When the students reach their second semester on the desk, however, they should be given a significant raise which acknowledges they have mastered a certain level of competency at the reference desk.

Knowing When to Refer to the Public Services Librarian

A pivotal skill for Reffies is recognizing when to stop attempting to answer a question and refer it to the public services librarian. There are several safety nets on which they may rely. For example, if they can tell immediately that the question asked involves extensive research, they might take the option of suggesting that the patron begin with a source like *The New Grove Dictionary of Music and Musicians*.[10] Then they should leave the patron's name and contact information in the log, and the public services librarian will contact the patron for a reference appointment. Another option is to fill out a "Request for Reference Assistance" form, and again, the public services librarian will then follow up with the patron. In general, if the Reffie is unable to answer the question in a reasonable amount of time (approximately fifteen minutes), they should be instructed to leave some sort of follow-up note for the public services librarian.

On occasion, Reffies may encounter complicated interactions or power dynamics in serving information needs of peers and faculty. For example, a classmate may ask for an analysis of a Beethoven quartet when the instructions from the professor were to do all analysis without consulting any sources. Or, a faculty member may request assistance when the Reffie is in the midst of helping a fellow student. In such situations, a Reffie should be encouraged to do what they can in the moment, but alert the public services librarian at the earliest convenience. Generally speaking, these situations will be few and far between, but do happen occasionally. It seems best to deal with each situation as it arises, being mindful of ethics and employing conflict mediation skills as needed.

Off-Desk Projects

For those reference assistants who want to work more than the requisite five hours per week, off-desk projects are an option. Tasks such as processing items requested from the collection through Interlibrary Loan are well-suited for students in these positions. Other significant off-desk projects might include adding records to local reference databases such as the *Oberlin College Song Index*,[11] annotating print reference works, for example. Any of these tasks help enrich the experience for the Reffie and, at the same time, frees the public services librarian for other work.

SUMMARY AND CONCLUSIONS

The reference assistant training program has worked well at Oberlin College for a number of years. It continues to be tweaked and modified, as trends in information needs evolve. The Reffies maintain positions that are intellectually stimulating and professionally applicable. The public services librarian's time can, therefore, be less structured and available for other opportunities such as collaborating with faculty on information literacy projects. Music students benefit by having access to knowledgeable peers who easily relate to their specific experience. At Oberlin, in spite of the fact that, as an undergraduate institution it does not have the option of calling on graduate students to work the reference desk, the Conservatory Library has moved beyond the notion of requiring the reference librarian to handle all the information needs for the community—which would be an impossible task.

It is worth noting that, in the last ten years at Oberlin, seven Reffies have gone on to "information-type" careers. Perhaps their time at the reference desk planted the seeds for further growth and development in this arena. When we are willing to nurture the potential of undergraduate music students, we can create a new model of service in which everyone benefits.

APPENDIX A: REFERENCE ASSISTANT INTERVIEW QUESTIONS

Candidate: _____
Year of Graduation: _____ Work Study: _____
Major: _____

1. Music History and Music Theory courses taken at Oberlin and elsewhere:
2. Language skills/computer skills:
3. Previous work experience:
4. Things in a previous job that you have done particularly well and enjoyed:
5. Things you value in a job and why:
6. Reasons that prompted you to consider applying for this job:
7. Previous library work experience:
8. Talk some about your use of the library for a particular project and how you found the process of research:

9. Areas of musical interest:
10. Concept of the ideal supervisor/supervisee relationship:
11. Explain an interpersonal conflict and how you handled it. If you could "do it over" is there anything you would do differently?
12. Personal strengths you bring to this position:
13. Things you feel most confident doing:
14. Are there any personality types or groups of people you find difficult to work with? How do you usually cope with them?

Comments:

APPENDIX B: CONTENTS OF REFERENCE TRAINING FOLDER

I. New Reference Assistant Training Schedule
II. New Student Procedures and Evaluation
III. Library Location Floor Plan
IV. "Searching Music on OBIS"[12] — located on the web at http://www.oberlin.edu/~library/OBIS/OBISmusic.html
V. Overview of LC and Dewey Classification (DDC) Schemes
VI. Database Structure
VII. Sample MARC record
VIII. 048 Number of Musical Instruments or Voices
IX. German used in Thematic Catalogs
X. Techniques for Searching Computer Databases
XI. Sample *FirstSearch Guides* (*WorldCat*, *RILM*)
XII. *Music Index*
XIII. Techniques for Using Search Engines
XIV. Song Translations Bibliography
XV. Song Search Bibliography
XVI. Finding Songs and Arias
XVII. Labs

Day 1: Ready Reference
New Grove, WWW
Day 2: Directories
Musical America,[13] Schirmer Guide,[14] WWW

Primary Sources

Day 3: Audiovisual Materials
OBIS, Schwann etc., Pipedreams,[15] Ethnomusicology catalog, Recordings catalog, Bio-bibliographies, Recital tapes and programs[16]
Day 4: Scores I
OBIS, OHIOLink, WorldCat, ILLs
Day 5: Scores II
Heyer,[17] New Grove/Thematic catalog—complete works
Day 6: Vocal Music
OBIS, Song Index, Spirituals Index,[18] New Grove Opera, WWW

Secondary Sources

Day 7: Information on a composition
Music Index,[19] IIMP,[20] RILM,[21] Diamond,[22] Wenk,[23] Bio-bibliographies
Day 8: Information on a person
OBIS, necrology (WWW), membership directories.
Day 9: Repertoire Guides
Repertoire guides, OBIS searching (Subject headings), Music Subject Headings[24]
Day 10: Big Concepts Day

APPENDIX C: NEW REFERENCE ASSISTANT TRAINING SCHEDULE

Meeting 1: Introduction to Reference Work

Work the reference desk for one hour!
General Orientation

1. Introductions, Tours
2. New Student Procedures and Evaluation
3. Library Locations Floor Plan

Overview of LC and Dewey Classification (DDC) Schemes
Discuss card catalogs: (1) Dewey, (2) Recordings, (3) Ethno
Discuss service philosophy and difficult user interactions

Meeting 2: Ready Reference and Quick Look-Ups

Ready Reference: *New Grove*, WWW (Lab I)

Meeting 3: Directories

Discuss Ready Reference Lab
Directories: *Musical America*, *Schirmer Guide*, *Guide to Music Schools in Canada and the U.S.*, WWW (Lab II)

Meeting 4: Recordings and Discographical Sources

Primary Sources
Discuss Directories Lab
Recordings: OBIS, *Schwann*, etc., Pipedreams, Ethnomusicology catalog, Recordings catalog, Bio-bibliographies, Recital tapes and programs (Lab III)

Meeting 5: Locating Scores

Discuss Recordings Lab
Scores I: OBIS, OHIOLink, *WorldCat*, ILLs (Lab IV)

Meeting 6: More on Locating Scores

Discuss Scores I Lab
Scores II: Heyer—monuments, *New Grove*/Thematic catalogs—complete works (Lab V)

Meeting 7: Issues Specific to Vocal Music

Discuss Scores II Lab
Vocal Music: OBIS, Song Index, Spirituals Index, *New Grove Opera*, and WWW. (Lab VI)

Meeting 8: Researching a Composition

Secondary Sources
Discuss Vocal Music Lab
Information on a Composition: *Music Index, IIMP, RILM*, Diamond, Wenk, and Bio-bibliographies. (Lab VII)
No training this week
Work the reference desk for two hours!

Meeting 9: Looking for Information about a Person

Discuss Information on a Piece Lab
Information on a Person: OBIS, necrology (WWW), and membership directories. (LabVIII)

Meeting 10: Locating Repertoire

Discuss Information on a Person Lab
Repertoire Guides: Repertoire guides, OBIS searching (Subject headings), Subject Index to Classical Music. (Lab IX)

Meeting 11: Review and Big Concepts

Discuss Repertoire Guides Lab
Big Concepts Day (Lab X)—brainstorm together
Work the reference desk for one hour!

Note: It is assumed that you will browse the pertinent section of the reference collection with each lab. Please bring any questions regarding that section of the collection to our discussions. I would also recommend that you read the reference log throughout your training and bring those questions to our discussions as well.

APPENDIX D: THE LABS

Lab I: Ready Reference Tools and Quick Look-Ups

Sources: *The New Grove Dictionary of Music and Musicians* (note: Please try to use both the web version and the print volumes), *The New Grove Dictionary of Musical Instruments* (4 vol.),[25] *The New Grove Dictionary of Opera* (4 vol.), *The New Grove Dictionary of American Music* (4 vol.),[26] *The Norton/Grove Concise Encyclopedia of Music*,[27] *The Norton/Grove Dictionary of Women Composers*,[28] *The Garland Encyclopedia of World Music*,[29] *The New Harvard Dictionary of Music*,[30] *Baker's Biographical Dictionary of Musicians*,[31] and the WWW.

1. Find an article on the music of the Tarahumara Indians of Mexico.
2. I'm playing a piece by the Czech composer Janácek called *Pohadka*. What does that word mean?
3. What is a *Theremin*?
4. At the top of a piece I'm working on is the indication M.M.=60. I know it means a metronome marking, but what exactly does it stand for?
5. What is the structure of the Catholic Mass?
6. When did Ethel Smyth write the *March of the Women?*
7. Find the dates and places of birth and death of the French organ builder Joseph Rabiny.
8. Who wrote *The Flight of the Bumble Bee?*
9. Find an article on Nguni music. Who are the Nguni and where do they live?
10. What is a "Scotch Snap"?

11. How do I cite a web page for a term paper?
12. Find a definition for the German musical term *Sprechgesang* or *Sprechstimme*. With the music of which composers is it associated?
13. What is the Köchel number of Mozart's Sinfonia Concertante for violin, viola, and orchestra?
14. I heard that Widor, the organ composer, wrote a cello sonata. What is its opus number?
15. Find an article on the Federal Music Project, a division of the Works Progress Administration (WPA) during Depression-era America.

Lab II: Directories

Sources: *Musical America: International Directory of the Performing Art* (Please explore both the web and print versions), *The Schirmer Guide to Schools of Music and Conservatories Throughout the World, Directory of Music Faculties in Colleges and Universities in the U.S. and Canada*[32], and the WWW.

1. Who is the principal clarinetist of the San Francisco Symphony?
2. Where does Joseph Schwantner teach?
3. At a recent concert, I met a musicology professor named Deborah Hayes, and I want to send her copies of some work I've been doing. How can I find her address?
4. Our trio wants to enter the chamber music competition that's held every year in Yellow Springs, Ohio. Where can I write for more information and an application?
5. My teacher mentioned that there was a Cleveland International Piano Competition. How can I get information about it?
6. When is the Boulder Bach Festival? Where can I write for a brochure listing performances for this year?

7. Which management agency handles conducting performances for JoAnn Falletta?
8. What is the New York Opera schedule this season?
9. What is the address for the Viola da Gamba Society of America?
10. Which schools offer a Master of Arts in Performing Arts Administration?
11. Locate information on music schools in Austria and Germany.

Lab III: Recordings and Discographical Sources

Sources: *Schwann Opus,*[33] *Schwann Artist,*[34] *Schwann Spectrum,*[35] *R.E.D. Classical Catalogue,*[36] *Bielefelder Katalog Klassik,*[37] OBIS, Pipedreams Index, Card Catalog, and Bio-bibliographies.

1. Find...
   a. a recording of *Ruckert Lieder.*
   b. a video of *Die Fledermaus.*
   c. a recording of Marilyn McDonald playing jazz.
   d. a recording of Jacqueline Du Pre playing Bruch's *Kol Nidrei.*
   e. a video of *Oedipus Rex* directed by Julie Taymor.
   f. a recording which has both Webern's op.30 and Ives's *The Unanswered Question.*
   g. a recording of Jorge Bolet playing Liszt's piano transcriptions of Schubert songs.
2. A book I was reading cited liner notes, but all it gave was the record number: sm3k 45845. What is the recording?
3. I'd like a recording of Beethoven's violin sonata in G major. I don't have the opus number, but I know he wrote it around 1815.
4. I heard that Oberlin performed Britten's *War Requiem* a couple of years ago. How can I find a tape of it?
5. Pipedreams aired an arrangement of Cole Porter's "Don't Fence Me In." What is the program number?

6. Has the Beaux Arts Trio recorded Ravel's Piano Trio? What is the label name and recording number?
7. What ensembles has Isaac Stern recorded with as a conductor?
8. I need a recording of keyboard sonatas by Galuppi. I think they were written in 1781. Is there a recording currently available?
9. I'd like to find a recording of Haydn's *La Vera Costanza* (Hob. XXVIII/8), but Oberlin doesn't own it. Is a recording available?
10. I need a recording of generic wedding music. How can I find one?
11. Driving back to campus, I heard this great recording of a Cèsar Franck orchestral work, conducted by Daniel Barenboim. I didn't quite catch the French title, but the announcer said it means "The Evil Hunter." If the library doesn't own this recording, I'd like to buy it. Can you help me identify it, and find a recording of it?

Lab IV: Locating Scores

Sources: OBIS, OhioLINK, and *WorldCat*.

1. Find . . .
    a. a score of *The Seasons* by three different composers.
    b. a score and parts for Pachelbel's Canon arranged for brass.
    c. a score of music by Margaret Ruthven Lang.
    d. a score of Ravel's Piano Concerto in G arranged for two pianos.
    e. a Christmas fake book.
    f. a score of Schubert's D.944 arranged for piano, 4-hands.
    g. parts for Beethoven's piano trio WoO 38.
    h. parts for Messiaen's *Quartet for the End of Time*.
    i. parts for Wolfgang Fortner's Serenade for flute, oboe, and bassoon.

Reference Assistants in the Music Library   115

    j. a Breitkopf and Härtel edition of C.P.E. Bach's Harp Sonata.
    k. a Henle edition of Beethoven's Horn Sonata.
    l. an orchestral score of Copland's Clarinet Concerto.
2. I need a copy of Ruth Crawford Seeger's *Let's Build a Railroad*, but Oberlin doesn't own it. Do any libraries in Ohio have it?
3. I'd like the score to *Mirabai Songs* by John Harbison. We own the piano/vocal edition, but I understand Harbison did an arrangement for alto flute, bass clarinet, percussion, harp, violin, viola, violoncello, and double bass. Could you help me find that?
4. A student orchestra will be performing Milhaud's *Maximillian Suite* next spring, and we need to order a score and parts. Who publishes this?
5. I heard both William Primrose and Lionel Tertis edited versions of the Brahms viola sonatas. Could you help me find them?

Lab V: More on Locating Scores

Sources: *Historical Sets, Collected Editions, and Monuments of Music* (Heyer), Thematic Catalogues, *Orchestral Excerpts: A Comprehensive Index*,[38] and *The New Grove Dictionary of Music and Musicians*.

1. Locate a score of Monteverdi's madrigal *Damigella tutta bella*.
2. Locate a score for C.P.E. Bach's Quartet a-moll for piano, flute, viola, and cello.
3. Locate a copy of the Montpellier Codex.
4. Have the complete works of John Dunstable been published? If so, where?
5. In which series has Telemann's Concerto a-moll für violine, streicher, und basso continue been published?
6. Which series in the Schubert Werke is for lieder? In which volume can I find *Die Schöne Müllerin*?

7. Where can one find a copy of William Billing's anthem *Peace?* Does the Conservatory Library have a copy?
8. Where in the new edition (*Neue Ausgabe*) of Mozart's complete works can one find his Requiem? Where can the same work be found in the old edition (*W. A. Mozart: Sämtliche werke*)?
9. Where in Hindemith's Collected Works can you find his Requiem?
10. Where can I find a score of the secular cantatas by Elizabeth Jacquet De La Guerre? Someone mentioned that Garland might have published it.
11. I need a Vivaldi piece, Pincherle 88. What's the RV number, and what is it scored for?
12. Where in the complete works can I find the Vivaldi Oboe Concerto RV 465?
13. I need a score of Handel's *Serse*, and I can't find a copy in OBIS. Where would I find it in the complete works?
14. I'm playing an audition in the spring, and I need the first violin parts of Mozart's Symphony #35 and Prokofiev's *Classical Symphony*. Could you help me find those?

Lab VI: Issues Specific to Vocal Music

Sources: Appropriate sources for this lab include: *Guide to Operatic Roles and Arias*,[39] *Word-by-Word Translations of Songs and Arias*,[40] *The Fischer-Dieskau Book of Lieder: the Original texts of Over Seven Hundred and Fifty Songs*,[41] and *Masters of the Italian Art Song: Word-by-Word and Poetic Translations of the Complete Songs for Voice and Piano*.[42] Additional sources are listed in the Oberlin Conservatory Library documents: *Song Search Bibliography*; *Song Translations Bibliography*; and *Finding Songs and Arias in the Oberlin Conservatory Library*.

I. Librettos and Synopses
   A. Find a libretto of *Akhnaten* by Philip Glass.
   B. Find a libretto of Wagner's Ring Cycle.

C. Find a synopsis of *Die Fledermaus* by Richard Strauss.
  D. Find a synopsis of *Madame Imperia*.
II. Translations
  A. Find a literal translation of Mahler's *Fünf Rückert Lieder.*
  B. Find a literal translation of "Les Papillons" by Chausson.
  C. Find an IPA translation of Mussorgsky's "Evening Prayer."
III. Scores—Opera
  A. Find a vocal score of *Four Saints in Three Acts.*
  B. Find a full orchestral score of *Don Giovanni.*
  C. Find a score of Tchaikovsky's *Eugene Onegin* with Cyrillic text.
IV. Scores—Lieder
  A. Find a score of Scarlatti's "Le Violette."
  B. Find a score of Schubert's "Trockne Blumen." Is it part of a song cycle? What is its Deutsch number? (Do not use the Song Index.)
  C. Find a score of "Peter Go Ring Dem Bells."
V. Arias and Characters
  A. Who wrote the aria "Amour, viens aider," and from which opera does it come?
  B. What opera has a character named "Lina"?
VI. Popular Songs
  A. When was "Little Brown Jug" written, and who revived it?
  B. I'm looking for a score of *Small Songs* by Carrie Jacobs-Bond. Who publishes them?
  C. I need to sing "Send in the Clowns" for an audition. What musical is it from, and who wrote it?
  D. I need a score of the song "Brother, can you spare a dime."

Lab VII: Researching a Composition

Sources: Appropriate sources for this lab may include indices (such as *Music Index, RILM,* and *IIMP*); composer bibliographies and catalogs in the ML134s; topic bibliographies in the ML128s; musical analysis bibliographies; *New Grove*; and OBIS.

I. Factual Information
   A. To whom did Beethoven dedicate his "Battle Symphony," *Wellingtons Sieg?*
   B. When was Rimsky-Korsakov's opera, *Sadko*, first performed?
   C. Dmitrii Shostakovich wrote the score for the film, *The Fall of Berlin*. When did the movie premiere?
   D. Who played flute in the premiere of Violet Archer's Sonata for Flute, Clarinet and piano in A?
   E. What is the Hoboken catalog number for Haydn's *Missa in Tempore Belli?* When was it composed? Where is the autograph manuscript located?
II. Analytical and Musicological Information
   A. Find an article on Chausson's songs.
   B. Are there any books on Messaien's *Quatuor pour la fin du temps?*
   C. I need to give a short pre-concert talk on Mozart's Viola Quintet in G minor, K. 516. Where could I find some basic information?
   D. For my midterm I have to write a short essay on Berlioz's *Symphonie Fantastique*. What sources would you suggest I use?
   E. I'm working on a ten- to fifteen-page paper on Britten's *Peter Grimes*. I need to find two books and three articles from refereed journals for my preliminary bibliography. Could you help me with this?
III. Reviews
   A. Find a review of Cecil Effinger's *Cantata for Easter* (1971).
   B. Find reviews of some recent recordings of Weill's Violin Concerto.
IV. Music in Print
   A. Are Arnold Schoenberg's *Organ Variations* still in print? If so, who publishes them?

Lab VIII: Looking for Information about a Person

Possible Sources: *The New Grove Dictionaries, The Norton/Grove Concise Encyclopedia of Music, The Norton/Grove Dictionary of Women Composers, The New Harvard Dictionary of Music, Baker's Biographical Dictionary of Musicians, Who's Who, Bio-bibliographies, Music Index, IIMP, RILM, newspaper indices, Schwann Opus, Directories from the "Directories File,"* OBIS, OHIOLink, *WorldCat* and the WWW.

I. Dates
   A. When was Herbert von Karajan born, and when did he die?
   B. When did Ross Lee Finney, an American composer, die?
   C. Is Dietrich Fischer-Dieskau still alive?
II. Obituaries
   A. Find obituaries for Leonard Bernstein, Nicholas Slonimsky, and Raymond Raspberry (d. 1995). Use at least two sources.
III. Basic Information
   A. Find a brief biography of Kirke Mechem, an American composer.
   B. I heard Steven Sondheim studied with Milton Babbitt. Is this true?
   C. Find a *Curriculum Vitae* of soprano Renee Fleming.
   D. I'm going to be in Massachusetts for Winter Term, and my teacher recommended I study with Peter Atkins, a horn player. I think he's a member of the International Horn Society. How can I get in touch with him?
   E. Where could I find a basic bibliography of works about Jean Sibelius?
IV. Information in Depth
   A. Could you help me find a book of Brahms's correspondence?
   B. I need to give an oral presentation on Carrie Jacobs-Bond. Where could I find a brief biographical article?

C. For my midterm project I have to write a five-page essay on Elliot Carter's compositional techniques. I'd like to find some of his own writings on his work, but I don't have time to read a lot of articles. Is there an annotated bibliography I could use?

D. I'm writing a ten- to fifteen-page paper on the Italian opera director, Franco Zeffirelli. I need to find two books and three articles for a preliminary bibliography. Could you help me find them?

Lab IX: Locating Repertoire

Sources: OBIS, *Music Subject Headings* by Hemmasi, Reference Sources in the ML128s, "048 Chart," "Synopsis of LC and DD Classification Systems."

I. OBIS
   Do a Word Search on the following terms to locate Subject Headings. List an appropriate LC subject heading.
   A. Mezzo songs.
   B. Trumpet orchestral studies.
   C. Big band recordings.
   D. Flute and clarinet duets.
   E. Music for jazz trombone.

II. OBIS: Subject Headings
   Locate an appropriate LC subject heading using 048 codes.
   A. Music for piano and organ.
   B. Music for three trumpets.
   C. Music for two violins and cello.
   D. Music for violin, cello, clarinet, and piano.
   E. Music for a soprano and orchestra.
   F. Songs for high voice and string quartet.

III. Printed Sources
   (Note: use various sources in Reference ML128s for this section.)
   A. Music for cello and tape.
   B. Piano music by Greek composers.

C. Easy etude/method books for flute.
   D. Organ music by women composers.
   E. Wedding music.
   F. I'm playing Schumann's Pappions, and I was wondering if there is any other music about butterflies?
   G. Latin-American choral music.
IV. Browsing the Shelves
   List LC and Dewey number areas from "Synopsis of LC and DDC Classification Systems."
   A. Where are the opera scores?
   B. Where are the string quartets?
   C. Where are the brass quintets?

Lab X: Review and Big Concepts

I. Review
   A. What does "rasg." stand for?
   B. Where does Susan McClary teach?
   C. I'd like to find some recordings of folk music from Ohio.
   D. Schubert's *Winterreise* has been arranged for voice and guitar. Could you help me find a score?
   E. I couldn't find a copy of Thomas Tallis' *Veni Redemptor* in OBIS. Is there anywhere else I could look?
   F. Besides Verdi's *Falstaff*, are there any other operas with a character named Falstaff?
   G. I'm looking for information on Mozart's six "Haydn Quartets."
   H. I'd like to find out about Evelyn Glennie, the percussionist.
   I. How could I find a list of twentieth-century harpsichord music?
II. Big Concepts
   A. Where could I find information on injury prevention for double bass players?
   B. I am writing a paper on the Kodaly method of teaching music. Where can I find articles on this? I'd especially like to find a bibliographical article.

C. How could I find out about current music copyright laws?
D. I work in the Conservatory PR office, and I have to find some reviews of books by conservatory faculty. I'm especially looking for Mr. Rothstein's *Phrase Rhythm in Tonal Music*.
E. I found this page of music lying by the copy machines, and I'd really like to know the composer and title. How could I find that information?
F. I'd like to find some information about a Riot Grrrls band named Bikini Kill. I know they avoid printed sources, so where could I look?
G. How could I find articles on hearing loss in musicians?
H. How could I find articles on Handel's use of the trumpet?
I. I'm working on my recital invitations, and I'd like to find some drawings of musical instruments. How should I go about looking for them?

APPENDIX E: PROFILE OF OBERLIN COLLEGE CONSERVATORY LIBRARY

The Conservatory Library offers service to the Oberlin Conservatory community of approximately six hundred twenty undergraduate students and a faculty of seventy-five. The Conservatory provides pre-professional training in music performance, composition, music education, music technology, music theory, and music history. Students may earn one or more of the undergraduate and graduate degrees: Bachelor of Music, Performance Diploma, Artist Diploma, Master of Music, Master of Music in Teaching, or Master of Music Education. In addition, the Conservatory Library serves approximately 2,000 students in the College of Arts and Sciences, which provides a rich curriculum in the humanities, social sciences, and sciences.

The Conservatory Library's collection exceeds 205,000 items, making it comparable to the largest music libraries in academic settings both public and private. The collection includes more than 58,000 sound recordings, over 96,000 musical scores, more than 51,000 books, and 220 periodical titles. Each year approximately 2,000 recordings, 3,300 scores, and 1,400 books are added. The Library's collection comprises a substantial foundation of Western art music from all historical periods, complete editions of the works of major composers, as well as an ever-growing collection in the areas of women musicians and American, ethnic, contemporary, jazz, folk, and popular music.

Additionally, some Conservatory Library materials reside in the Department of Special Collections in the central library located in Mudd Center. The Violin Society of America/H. K. Goodkind Collection, for example, contains extensive monographic and journal literature on the construction, performance, teaching, collecting, and playing of stringed instruments.

The Conservatory Library has a comprehensive plan in place in order to serve the needs of its users. It is a fully-functioning library with technical services (cataloging, acquisitions, processing and preparations), collection development, and management operating on site along with a complete offering of public services (circulation, reserve, reference and instruction). While much of the responsibility for reference service falls to the public services librarian, the student staff of reference assistants is integral to every aspect of the service offered.

APPENDIX F: INFORMATION LITERACY AT OBERLIN COLLEGE CONSERVATORY LIBRARY

The public services librarian may also provide course-integrated instructional service designed to help students use the library and the Internet for research or studio assignments. This not only provides students with the specific skills needed to complete assignments, it prepares them to make effective lifelong use of information sources and systems. While various library instructional sessions are planned for groups representing the private studio, music education, jazz studies, conducting or the academic classroom, the most noted instruction programs in the conservatory are with Music History 101[43] and Opera Theater 202/203.[44]

Reference Internship

For those Reffies who are seriously interested in the music library profession, Oberlin College Conservatory Library offers a summer internship. This position is funded by the Summer Programs Office of the Conservatory of Music specifically to provide reference and research assistance in the Conservatory of Music Library for participants in Oberlin's summer music institutes including: the Baroque Performance Institute, the Oberlin Flute Institute, the Institute of Vocal Performance Pedagogy, and Workshops in Electronic and Computer Music. Participants in summer programs range from musically talented high school students, through accomplished adult students, to practicing professional performers and teachers. Institute participants total well over four hundred musicians each summer.

NOTES

1. A former reference assistant, Michael Fenton, contributed to this chapter as well as collaborated in the editing and revising of the labs. The author would also like to acknowledge the work of her predecessor, Carolyn Rabson, who initiated this program.

2. See Appendix E for an overview of Oberlin College Conservatory Library that provided the original setting for this program's inspiration and development.

3. At Oberlin, these student employees can record as many as 5,000 responses to questions per year.

4. See also Appendix F, Information Literacy at Oberlin College. Conservatory Library.

5. Given that these positions are both highly visible and desirable at the Oberlin Conservatory Library, most applicants are aware of the nature of the position prior to application.

6. At Oberlin, most Reffies are selected based upon their application and interview. A few, however, have participated in the reference assistant training as a result of the Oberlin College Diversity Intern Program. In 2001, Oberlin College Library was awarded a National Leadership Grant from the Institute of Museum and Library Services, a federal grant-making agency located in Washington, D.C. The grant funded a two-year project to establish a program for recruiting students from diverse backgrounds into the library profession by offering undergraduate fellowships and graduate internships in combination with mentoring by library staff and work experience in the college library. Oberlin College library staff members collaborated to create a curriculum designed to introduce the interns to libraries and librarianship.

7. The 048 field in the MARC record is used to identify the instrumentation of a score or musical recording. Local indexing of the 048 field is especially useful when Library of Congress Subject Headings (LCSH) provide inadequate information. For example, *Two Latin Elegies* by John McCabe is scored for counter-tenor, treble/tenor recorder, violoncello and harpsichord, with optional cup bells. One of the LCSH used for this piece is "Songs (High voice) with instrumental ensemble." Two or more instruments (except 2 keyboard instruments) that accompany vocal works are called "instrumental ensemble." Searchable access to the 048 field allows the user to search by specific instrumentation, and searching by number of performers as well. For example, the user has access to the following information: vh01 (vh=high voice; 01=one performer) wh01 (recorder—one performer) sc01 (violoncello—one performer) kc01 (harpsichord—one performer).

8. For the most part, the questions that illustrate the Labs in Appendix D have been derived from actual reference queries encountered at the Oberlin Conservatory Library.

9. During one semester at the Oberlin Conservatory, the entire staff wrote haiku in the log between reference questions.

10. *The New Grove Dictionary of Music and Musicians*, 2nd ed., ed. Stanley Sadie; John Tyrrell, executive editor. (New York: Grove, 2001).

11. This tool is a FileMaker Pro database that indexes 46,000+ songs in anthologies held by the Conservatory Library.

12. OBIS, the Oberlin Bibliographic Information System, is Oberlin's online catalog.

13. Musical America: International Directory of the Performing Arts. (Great Barrington, Mass.: ABC Leisure Magazines).

14. Nancy Uscher. *The Schirmer Guide to Schools of Music and Conservatories Throughout the World.* (New York: Schirmer Books; London: Collier Macmillan, 1988).

15. This tool is a FileMaker Pro database of selected audio cassettes of Pipedreams®, the American Public Radio program (created by Oberlin alumnus Michael Barone) devoted to the organ and its literature.

16. Oberlin College. Conservatory of Music. *Programs of Concerts and Recitals.* (Oberlin, Ohio: Oberlin College).

17. Anna Harriet Heyer. *Historical Sets, Collected Editions, and Monuments of Music: a Guide to Their Contents*, 3rd ed. (Chicago: American Library Association, 1980).

18. Kathleen A. Abromeit. *An Index to African-American Spirituals for the Solo Voice.* (Westport, Conn.: Greenwood Press, 1999).

19. *The Music Index Online* [computer file]. (Warren, Mich.: Harmonie Park Press).

20. *International Index to Music Periodicals* [computer file]: IIMP. (Alexandria, Va.: Chadwyck-Healey Inc.).

21. *RILM Abstracts of Musical Literature* [electronic resource]. (New York: RILM).

22. Harold J. Diamond. *Music Analyses: an Annotated Guide to the Literature.* (New York: Schirmer Books: Maxwell Macmillan International; Toronto: Collier Macmillan Canada, 1991).

23. Arthur B. Wenk. *Analyses of Nineteenth- and Twentieth-Century Music, 1940–1985.* (Boston: Music Library Association, 1987).

24. Harriette Hemmasi. *Music Subject Headings: Compiled from Library of Congress Subject Headings,* 2nd. ed. (Lake Crystal, Minn.: Soldier Creek Press, 1998).

25. *The New Grove Dictionary of Musical Instruments,* ed. Stanley Sadie. (London: Macmillan; New York: Grove's Dictionaries of Music, 1984).

26. *The New Grove Dictionary of American Music,* ed. H. Wiley Hitchcock and Stanley Sadie. (London: Macmillan; New York: Grove's Dictionaries of Music, sole distributor, 1986).

27. *The Norton/Grove Concise Encyclopedia of Music,* ed. Stanley Sadie; assistant editor, Alison Latham. (New York: W. W. Norton, 1988).

28. *The Norton/Grove Dictionary of Women Composers,* ed. Julie Anne Sadie & Rhian Samuel. (New York; London: W. W. Norton, 1994).

29. *The Garland Encyclopedia of World Music.* [advisory editors, Bruno Nettl and Ruth M. Stone; founding editors, James Porter and Timothy Rice]. (New York: Garland Pub., 1998–).

30. *The New Harvard Dictionary of Music,* ed. Don Michael Randel. (Cambridge, Mass.: Belknap Press of Harvard University Press, 1986).

31. *Baker's Biographical Dictionary of Musicians.* Nicolas Slonimsky, editor emeritus; Laura Kuhn, Baker's series advisory editor. (New York: Schirmer Books, 2001).

32. *Directory of Music Faculties in Colleges and Universities, U.S. and Canada.* (Binghamton, N.Y.: College Music Society).

33. *Schwann Opus.* (Santa Fe, N.M.: Stereophile, Inc., 1992–2001).

34. *Schwann Artist: America's Guide to Classical Performers.* (Santa Fe, N.M.: Stereophile, Inc., 1996–).

35. *Schwann Spectrum.* (Santa Fe, N.M.: Stereophile, Inc., 1992–).

36. *R.E.D. Classical Catalogue.* Master ed. (London: Retail Entertainment Data, 1996–).

37. *Bielefelder Katalog Klassik.* (Karlsruhe, Germany: G. Braun).

38. Carolyn Rabson. *Orchestral Excerpts: A Comprehensive Index.* (Berkeley, Calif.: Fallen Leaf Press, 1993).

39. Richard Boldrey. *Guide to Operatic Roles and Arias.* (Dallas: Pst...Inc., 1994).

40. Berton Coffin, Werner Singer and Pierre Delattre. *Word-by-Word Translations of Songs and Arias.* 2 vols. (Metuchen, N.J.: Scarecrow, 1972 and 1966).

41. Dietrich Fischer-Dieskau. *The Fischer-Dieskau Book of Lieder: The Original Texts of over Seven Hundred and Fifty Songs.* (New York: Knopf, 1977).

42. Timothy Le Van. *Masters of the Italian Art Song: Word-by-Word and Poetic Translations of the Complete Songs for Voice and Piano.* (Metuchen, N.J.: Scarecrow, 1990).

43. Music History 101 is a survey of the major developments in the history of Western music including jazz, vernacular music, electronic and computer music, and an introduction to ethnomusicology. This course serves as a prerequisite to other music history courses. One component of

this class is a library project, which serves as 10 percent of the semester grade. It is possible for a student to test out of MH101, but that student must then either pass a library project exemption exam or complete the library project in order to graduate.

44. This information literacy project was the result of a grant from the Andrew W. Mellon Foundation. For complete information regarding this grant, consult http://www.denison.edu/collaborations/ohio5/grant. The work for this grant began during spring semester 2001 and was taken to the classroom during fall 2001 and spring 2002. While the primary work on the grant was accomplished through collaboration between Victoria Vaughan and Kathy Abromeit, Eric Einhorn was responsible for web development (http://www.oberlin.edu/opera/), and Leslie Roberts was the research assistant.

BIBLIOGRAPHY

Abromeit, Kathleen A. *An Index to African-American Spirituals for the Solo Voice*. Westport, Conn.: Greenwood Press, 1999.

Baker's Biographical Dictionary of Musicians. Nicolas Slonimsky, editor emeritus; Laura Kuhn, Baker's series advisory editor. New York: Schirmer Books, 2001.

Bielefelder Katalog Klassik. Karlsruhe, Germany: G. Braun.

Boldrey, Richard. *Guide to Operatic Roles and Arias*. Dallas: Pst...Inc., 1994.

Coffin, Berton, Werner Singer, and Pierre Delattre. *Word-by-Word Translations of Songs and Arias*. 2 vols. Metuchen, N.J.: Scarecrow, 1972 & 1966.

Diamond, Harold J. *Music Analyses: An Annotated Guide to the Literature*. New York: Schirmer Books: Maxwell Macmillan International; Toronto: Collier Macmillan Canada, 1991.

Directory of Music Faculties in Colleges and Universities, U.S. and Canada. Binghamton, N.Y.: College Music Society.

Fischer-Dieskau, Dietrich. *The Fischer-Dieskau Book of Lieder: The Original Texts of Over Seven Hundred and Fifty Songs*. New York: Knopf, 1977.

The Garland Encyclopedia of World Music. Advisory editors, Bruno Nettl and Ruth M. Stone; founding editors, James Porter and Timothy Rice. New York: Garland Pub., 1998–.

Hemmasi, Harriette. *Music Subject Headings: Compiled from Library of Congress Subject Headings.* 2nd ed. Lake Crystal, Minn.: Soldier Creek Press, 1998.

Heyer, Anna Harriet. *Historical Sets, Collected Editions, and Monuments of Music: A Guide to Their Contents.* 3rd ed. Chicago: American Library Association, 1980.

International Index to Music Periodicals [computer file]: IIMP. Alexandria, Va.: Chadwyck-Healey Inc.

Le Van, Timothy. *Masters of the Italian Art Song: Word-by-Word and Poetic Translations of the Complete Songs for Voice and Piano.* Metuchen, N.J. & London: Scarecrow Press, Inc., 1990.

The Music Index Online [computer file]. Warren, Mich.: Harmonie Park Press.

Musical America. International Directory of the Performing Arts. Great Barrington, Mass.: ABC Leisure Magazines.

The New Grove Dictionary of American Music. Edited by H. Wiley Hitchcock and Stanley Sadie. London: Macmillan; New York: Grove's Dictionaries of Music, sole distributor, 1986.

The New Grove Dictionary of Music and Musicians. 2nd ed. Edited by Stanley Sadie; John Tyrrell, executive editor. New York: Grove, 2001.

The New Grove Dictionary of Musical Instruments. Edited by Stanley Sadie. London: Macmillan; New York: Grove's Dictionaries of Music, 1984.

The New Harvard Dictionary of Music. Edited by Don Michael Randel. Cambridge, Mass.: Belknap Press of Harvard University Press, 1986.

The Norton/Grove Concise Encyclopedia of Music. Edited by Stanley Sadie; assistant editor, Alison Latham. New York: W.W. Norton, 1988.

The Norton/Grove Dictionary of Women Composers. Edited by Julie Anne Sadie & Rhian Samuel. New York; London: W. W. Norton, 1994

Oberlin College. Conservatory of Music. *Programs of Concerts and Recitals.* [Oberlin, Ohio]: Oberlin College.

Rabson, Carolyn. *Orchestral Excerpts: A Comprehensive Index.* Berkeley, Calif.: Fallen Leaf Press, 1993.

R.E.D. Classical Catalogue. Master ed. London: Retail Entertainment Data, 1996–.

RILM Abstracts of Musical Literature [electronic resource]. New York: RILM.

Schwann Opus. Santa Fe, N.M.: Stereophile, Inc., 1992–2001.

Schwann Spectrum. Santa Fe, N.M.: Stereophile, Inc., 1992– .

Uscher, Nancy. *The Schirmer Guide to Schools of Music and Conservatories Throughout the World.* New York: Schirmer Books; London: Collier Macmillan, 1988.

Wenk, Arthur B. *Analyses of Nineteenth- and Twentieth-Century Music, 1940–1985.* Boston: Music Library Association, 1987.

Index

Italic page numbers refer to tables and figures.

academic librarians. *See* librarians
ACRL. *See* Association of College and Research Libraries
ACRL BIS. *See* Association of College and Research Libraries' Bibliographic Instruction Section
archives, 60; at Eastman School of Music, 96n21
articles, journal, 56; citing, 59
assessment: characteristics of, 22; games, 35–43, 44; in backward design, 17; in information literacy, 21–24, 44; interactions as, 22–23; low-stakes writing, 23–24; questions, designing for, 23–24; of resources, 56–57
assignments: critical thinking, 33; designing, 26–27, 32; example, for music encyclopedia, 27–30; example, for website evaluation, 30–32; facilitated learning in, 26–27; objective portion, 32, 33; paper preparation, 49; reflective portion, 33; subjective portion, 32, 33
assistants, reference. *See* reference assistants
Association of College and Research Libraries (ACRL), competency standards, 4–5
Association of College and Research Libraries' Bibliographic Instruction Section (BIS), vii

backward design, 17
"Bibliographic Competencies for Music Students at an Undergraduate Level," vii, viii
bibliographic instruction. *See* information literacy
bibliographies: as resource, 16, 17; as sample assignment, 87–88; composer, 55–56; preliminary literature, 50, 81

Index

bibliography class. *See* research course
BIS. *See* Association of College and Research Libraries' Bibliographic Instruction Section
Bluff and Bluster, 35–38
books, 55, 56; citing, 59; sample assignment, 88–89

collected works, 58. *See also* editions of music
competencies, of information literacy, 4–11, 43; affective, 5, 6; games that assess, 35–43; general, 5, 6; library instruction, 6–11; standards, ACRL, 4–5; time recommendations, *19*; transference of, 16
composer bibliographies, 55–56. *See also* bibliographies
contemporary editions, 59. *See also* editions of music
copyright issues, 61
course: objectives, 14, 43; papers. *See* research papers
courses: mini, 3, 18; semester-long, 3, 18. *See also* research course
Craft of Research, 94n3–95n3
critical editions, 58. *See also* editions of music

dictionaries: as instruction resource, 16, 17; as research paper resource, 55–56; citing, 59; game, 35–38; sample assignment, 85–87

digital resources, viii. *See also* resources
"A Directory of Instruction Programs in the Midwest," vii
discographies, 16
discussions, 49
dissertations. *See* books
drafting, 50–51, 81, 82–84

Eastman School of Music, 94n1
editions of music, 57–59; citing, 59; contemporary, 59; sample assignments, 89–94
electronic databases, 55–56; sample assignment, 88–89
encyclopedias: as instruction resource, 16–17; as research paper resource, 55–56; citing, 59; sample assignments, 27–30, 85–87
evaluation. *See* assessment

facilitated learning, 26–27, 44; examples of, 26–32; online tutorials, 33–35
Fenton, Michael, 124n1
footnotes, 50, 60, 81–82
free writing, 23–24

games, as learning tools, 35, 44
grading, 61; sample, 66

indexes, 16, 17
information literacy, 1–45; as a job requirement for librarians, 1–2; assessment of, 21–24; assignments, 26–33; at Oberlin

College Conservatory Library, 123–24; at University of Hawaii at Manoa, 3–4; competencies of, 4–11, 43; concept of, viii, 18; course objectives, 14; history of, vii–viii; home use, result on, viii; methodology, 20–21; resources to teach, 15–17, 43; seven Cs of, 11–12; syllabus, 12–14; technology and, 24–26; timing, 17–20, 44; types of, 3
interviewing: reference assistants, 101; sample questions, 106–7
introduction, writing, 50–51, 81, 82–84

journals, as form of low-stakes writing, 24; electronic, 24

learning objectives, 48; sample, 69–78
librarians: benefits of teaching research course, 65–66; positions, 1; teaching bibliographic instruction, vii, 1–2; teaching research course, 61–63. *See also* personnel; public services librarians
library catalogs: as instruction resource, 16; as research paper resource, 54–55
literature, music, 55–57
low-stakes writing, 23–24

manuscripts, 57–58. *See also* editions of music
mechanics. *See* writing mechanics

mental dazzle, 15–16
methodology, of teaching skills, 20–21
MLA. *See* Music Library Association
music bibliography class. *See* research course
music editions. *See* editions of music
music librarians. *See* librarians
Music Library Association (MLA): influence on group instruction, vii; midwest chapter, vii; music literature, 55–57; *Notes*, vii, viii
music research course. *See* research course

objectives: as part of backward design, 17; course, 14, 43; learning, 48; sample learning objectives, 69–78
online catalogs. *See* library catalogs;
online databases, 55–56; sample assignment, 88–89
online resources, vii–viii. *See also* resources
online tutorials, 33–35. *See also* tutorials
outline, 50–51, 81, 82–84

paper preparation assignments, 49, 50–51; bibliographies, 50, 81; drafting, 50–51, 81, 82–84; footnoting, 50, 60, 81–82; introduction, 50–51, 81, 82–84; outline, 50–51, 81, 82–84;

quotation, 50, 60, 81–82; sample assignments, 50–51, 81; summarizing, 50, 60, 81–82
papers. *See* research papers
performance editions. *See* editions of music
periodicals, 55, 56
personnel, 61–63; qualifications for, 61; team teaching, 63; workload issues, 62–63. *See also* librarians; public services librarians
preliminary work, 49
presentations, 3
printed editions, 57–58. *See also* editions of music

quoting, 50, 60, 81–82

Rabson, Carolyn, 124n1
reference assistants: bibliography for, 128–30; hiring, 101; interviewing, 101; in music library, 99–130; Oberlin College's program, 105–6; logging questions at reference desk, 103–4; off-desk projects, 105; overview of services, 99–100; qualifications, 101; referring questions to public services librarians, 104–5; sample interview questions, 106–7; sample labs, 111–22; sample training folder, 107–8; sample training schedule, 108–11; selecting, 100–101; selecting, at Oberlin College, 125; shadowing, 103; training, 101–5; training labs, 102–3; working at the reference desk, 103–4
reference internship, 124
reference services, 99–100
reference works, 16
reffies. *See* reference assistants
research: argument, 53–54; audience for, 52; defining, 51–52; process of, 49–50, 51–54; warrants, 54
research course: assignments for, 49; benefits to librarian, 65–66; benefits to student, 65; class discussions in, 49, 51; class scheduling, 64; class size, 63–64; grading, 61; in graduate curriculum, 64–65; issues teaching, 47–48; learning objectives, 48; personnel, 61–63; sample general information, 66–69; sample materials for, 66–94; sample schedule for class, 69–78; teaching, 47–97; textbooks, 51; traditional approach to, 47. *See also* research; research papers
research papers: copyright issues, 61; for music research course, 48–54; inappropriate resources for, 52; performance of, 51; preliminary work for, 49; preparation assignments, 49; research argument, 53–54; research process, 49–52; sample description, 78–81; thesis,

53–54; topics for, 48–49, 52–53; warrants, 54; writing mechanics, 59–60. *See also* research; research course

resources: citing, 59–60; class size effect on, 64; evaluation of, viii, 5, 56; for research paper, 54–59; inappropriate, 52; limiting, 16; too many, 15–16; types of, 16

Scavenger Hunt: as learning tool, 38–43; sample questions, 40–43

schedule: sample, for research assistant training, 108–11; sample, for research course, 69–78

scheduling, class, 64

seven Cs of information literacy, 11–12, 14

shadowing, 103

size of class, 63–64

special collections, 60; at Eastman School of Music, 96

student assistants. *See* reference assistants

summarizing, 50, 60, 81–82

syllabus, 43; brief vs. detailed, 13; developing, 12–14; guidelines for, 12; sample, 66–78

teachers. *See* librarians; personnel

teaching venues, 3

team teaching, 63; at Eastman School of Music, 96

technology, 24–26, 44; assessing abilities, 25; impact on librarians' jobs, 1; teaching in computer labs, 25–26

textbooks: choosing, 51; sample, 67–68

thematic catalogs, 55, 56, 57–58; sample assignment, 88

thesis: for research paper, 53–54; warrants, 53–54

timing, 17–18, 20; backward design, 17; recommendations for competencies, *19*

topics, 52–53

transference, of competencies, 16

tutorials: as teaching format, 3. *See also* online tutorials

University of Hawaii at Manoa, 44n2: approach to teaching, 3–4; library instruction competencies developed by, 6–11

warrants: assumed, 54; explicit, 54; of research argument, 53–54

websites, 30–32

worksheet, 56–57; sample, 84–85

World Wide Web, viii

writing mechanics, 59–60; citing sources, 59–60; footnoting, 60; quoting, 60; summarizing, 60

About the Authors and Editor

Gregg S. Geary teaches courses in scholarship, libraries, and technology to freshmen music and non-music majors and library management to graduate students at the University of Hawaii at Manoa, where he is head of the Sinclair Library and music librarian.

Laura M. Snyder is head of research and instructional services at the main library of the University of Houston. She has also held positions in music libraries, including Indiana University, St. Olaf College, the Oberlin College & Conservatory libraries, and the Sibley Music Library at the Eastman School of Music.

Kathleen A. Abromeit is the public services librarian at Oberlin Conservatory Library. She formerly held music library positions at Morris County Library in New Jersey and Wright State University in Ohio. She is the author of *An Index to African-American Spirituals for the Solo Voice*, along with numerous articles and reviews, and is involved in information literacy initiatives.

Deborah Campana is conservatory librarian at Oberlin Conservatory Library and serves on the board of directors of the American Music Center. As former music public services librarian at Northwestern University, she taught a graduate level course in music bibliography and oversaw instructional offerings given by the music library.

Made in the USA
Lexington, KY
25 November 2014